Mexifornia

Mexifornia
A State of Becoming

VICTOR DAVIS HANSON

ENCOUNTER BOOKS
NEW YORK AND LONDON

First published in 2003 by Encounter Books, an activity of Encounter for Culture and Education, Inc., a nonprofit tax exempt corporation.

Encounter Books website address: www.encounterbooks.com

Manufactured in the United States and printed on acid-free paper.

The paper used in this publication meets the minimum requirements of ANSI/NISO Z39.48-1992 (R 1997) (*Permanence of Paper*).

SECOND EDITION

Library of Congress Cataloging-in-Publication Data
Hanson, Victor Davis.
Mexifornia : a state of becoming / Victor Davis Hanson. — 2nd ed.
   p.   cm.
     ISBN-13: 978-1-59403-217-2 (pbk. : alk. paper)
     ISBN-10: 1-59403-217-3 (pbk. : alk. paper)
     1. Mexican Americans—California—Social conditions.   2. Mexican Americans—Government policy—California.   3. Immigrants—Government policy—California.   4. California—Emigration and immigration.   5. Mexico—Emigration and immigration.   6. California—Ethnic relations.   7. California—Social conditions.   8. Popular culture—California.   9. Hanson, Victor Davis.   10. Selma (Calif.)—Biography. I. Title.
F870.M5H37 2007
305.868'720794—dc22
2007021166

10 9 8 7 6 5 4 3 2 1

For my Classics students
at California State University, Fresno, 1984–2003

Contents

Preface to the Second Edition

Mexifornia IS AN EXTENDED essay akin to a memoir, not a scholarly, footnoted study of the economics and demography of illegal immigration. Yet nothing I have seen or experienced or read in the academic literature since the book's first publication has made me regret a single argument. On the contrary, much that has transpired in that time has bolstered what I learned firsthand growing up and living in central California.

Mexifornia came out during California's gubernatorial recall campaign of autumn 2003. The public was furious about massive debts, but also angry that the embattled Governor Gray Davis had appeased both employers and the more radical Hispanic politicians of the California legislature on the issue of illegal immigration. His legislation allowing driver's licenses for illegal aliens had already passed both houses of the state government. So it was no wonder that the book sometimes found its way into political debate, in both its high and low forms. For example, circulating on the Internet was a close facsimile of a California driver's license with a picture of a Mexican bandit (the gifted actor Alfonso Bedoya in *The Treasure of the Sierra Madre*). The mock license had a demeaning height (5'4"), weight ("too much"), and sex ("mucho"). "Mexifornia" was emblazoned across the top where "California" usually is stamped on the license.

Since the publication of *Mexifornia*, I have discussed the book's merits in hundreds of radio appearances, and in formal debates with reasonable critics such as Bernardo Mendez, the Mexican trade and press consul in San Francisco, and the essayist Richard Rodriguez. At lectures on university campuses, I have been shouted down by disruptive hecklers. There was an especially unpleasant experience at the University of Oregon on February 11, 2004, when protestors took over the first row of seats, waving placards during my speech and blocking the audience's view—without any remonstration from university officials.

In heated debates, I was often asked, "Why did you have to write this book?" We now forget that just a few years earlier—in the age of rolling amnesty, bilingual education and NAFTA exuberance—the status of millions of Mexican nationals in our midst was mostly a taboo subject. Anyone who wrote a book with a title like *Mexifornia* would have been considered an unhinged zealot, or at best a nagging Cassandra. "Mexifornia," in fact, was originally a term of approbation used by activists who were enthusiastic about California's changing demography; yet the left considered the book's title, as well as its arguments, to be unduly harsh to newcomers from Mexico. The right, on the other hand, welcomed the book as giving long-overdue attention to a scandal ignored by the mainstream Republican Party.

Fast-forward four years, and the climate has radically changed. Today the arguments of *Mexifornia*—close the borders, return to the melting pot, offer earned citizenship to most aliens in exchange for acceptance of English and American culture—seem almost tame. In 2002, when I began writing the book, no one thought that the U.S. Congress would vote to erect a wall along the border with Mexico. Now there is grumbling that the signed legislation entails only 700 miles of fencing instead of covering the entire 1,950-mile border. Deportation was once an unimaginable response to the problem of millions here illegally. Now its practicality, rather than its morality, appears to be the main point of contention in congressional debates. The attempt by Chicano activists in

California to banish the descriptive term "illegal alien" in favor of the politically correct "undocumented worker" has failed, along with state-mandated bilingual education and racial preferences. Efforts to demonize opponents of open borders as "anti-immigrant" or "nativist" have had only a marginal effect in stifling debate. The old utopian talk of a new borderless zone of dual cultures, spreading out on both sides of a disappearing boundary, has given way to reexamination of NAFTA and its facilitation of the cross-border flow of goods and services—along with illegal aliens and drugs.

Why have the terms of the debate over illegal immigration moved so markedly to the right since *Mexifornia* first appeared?

We return always to the question of numbers. While it is true that no one knows exactly how many are here illegally from Mexico and Latin America, estimates of eleven or twelve million illegal aliens—with half a million to one million arriving per year—are often accepted as reasonable by both sides in the debate. It is plausible that an additional three or four million illegal aliens have entered the country since *Mexifornia* was first published. The result of such staggering numbers is that aliens now are not just a presence in California or the American Southwest, but frequently appear at Home Depot parking lots in the Midwest, emergency rooms in New England, and construction sites in the Carolinas. This proliferation makes the issue an American rather than merely a Californian or Arizonian concern—and reifies the warnings at the end of the book. What was once true of California specifically is now a national problem.

Numbers are at the crux of the quandary over illegal immigration. In the 1970s, when there were perhaps a few million illegal immigrants residing in the United States, their unassimilated presence was hardly noticed. Most Americans assumed that the formidable powers of integration and popular culture would continue to incorporate any distinctive ethnic enclave, as had been done so successfully with past generations who arrived in large numbers from Europe, Asia or Latin America. But when over ten million came north from Mexico in little more than a decade—the great majority without English, a high school education or legality—entire apartheid communities began springing up in the American Southwest.

As I warned in *Mexifornia*, the debate will no longer split across liberal/conservative, Republican/Democrat, or even "white/brown" fault lines. Instead, class considerations increasingly divide Americans on the issue—as does the public recognition of cynicism on the part of the employer and Chicano lobbies. The majority of middle-class and poor whites, Asians, African-Americans and Hispanics wish to close the borders. They see few advantages in cheap service labor since they are not so likely to employ it to mow their lawns, watch their kids or clean their houses. Because the less well off eat out less often, use hotels infrequently and don't periodically remodel their homes, the economic advantages of inexpensive, off-the-books illegal alien labor are not readily apparent.

But the downside surely is. Truck drivers, carpenters, janitors and gardeners—unlike lawyers, doctors, actors, writers and professors—feel their jobs are threatened, or at least their wages lowered, by cheaper rival workers from Oaxaca or Jalisco. Americans who live in communities where thousands of illegal aliens have settled are likely to lack the money to move when Spanish-speaking students flood the schools and gangs proliferate. Poorer Americans of all ethnic backgrounds acknowledge that poverty provides no exemption from mastering English, so they wonder why the same is not true for incoming Mexican nationals.

The class division explains the anomaly of the *Wall Street Journal* op-ed pages echoing the arguments of the elite Chicano studies professors. Both tend to caricature and scorn the far less affluent Minutemen and English-only activists, in part because they do not experience firsthand the problems associated with illegal immigration, but instead find the presence of millions of aliens to be conducive to their own contrasting agendas. Indeed, anytime an alien crosses the border *legally*, fluent in English, and with a high school diploma, La Raza and the corporate farm or construction company alike lose a constituent.

The question of fairness about who is allowed into the United States is another source of public discontent—especially when almost 70 percent of all immigrants, legal and illegal, arrive from Mexico alone. Asians, for example, are puzzled as to why their relatives wait years for official approval to enter the country, while Mexican nationals come across the border illegally, counting on rolling amnesties to obtain citizenship. One of the unforeseen consequences of publishing *Mexifornia* was the great number of Southeast Asians and Punjabis who contacted me, asking for help with relatives caught in immigration limbo and red tape—as if pointing out what was wrong with the present corrupt and broken system meant that I had any expertise or influence in navigating anyone through it.

Meanwhile, the ripples of September 11—whether seen in the arrests of dozens of potential saboteurs here in America, or in the terrorist bombings in Madrid and London—remind Americans that their enemies can only do harm by stealthily entering the United States. It makes little sense to screen tourists, inspect cargo containers, and check the passenger lists of incoming flights when our border with an untrustworthy Mexico remains porous. While it may be true that the opponents of illegal immigration have used the post-9/11 fear of terrorism to further their own agenda of closing the border with Mexico, they are absolutely correct that presently the easiest way for jihadist cells to cross into the United States is overland from the south.

Other recent events have also helped steer the debate rightward. In the last decade, the United States has had bitter experiences with sectarianism and ethnic chauvinism abroad. There was the Hutu-Tutsi bloodbath in Rwanda, followed by the unraveling of Yugoslavia into Croatian, Serbian and Albanian camps. Now almost daily we hear of Pashtun-Tajik-Uzbek hatred among the multifarious warring clans in Afghanistan, and the ongoing mayhem between Kurds, Shiites and Sunnis in Iraq. When we are spending blood and treasure abroad to encourage the melting pot and national unity, why would anyone wish to foster tribalism or ethnic separatism here in the United States?

All during the 1990s, blue-state America offered up the European Union as the proper postmodern antidote to the United States. But the EU's statist and undemocratic tendencies, sluggish economic growth, high unemployment, falling demography and unsustainable entitlement commitments have resulted in much popular discontent, while its unassimilated Muslim minorities have added more tinder to the fire. The riots in France, the support for jihadism among Pakistanis in London, and the demands of Islamists in Scandinavia, Germany and the Netherlands do not encourage Americans to let in greater numbers of largely poor illegal immigrants who will advance the loud agendas of their sponsors, or to embrace the multicultural salad bowl over the distinctive American melting pot.

Then there were the demonstrations here in the United States in April–May 2006, when nearly half a million protestors took to the streets of our largest cities, from Chicago to Los Angeles. Previously naïve Americans had assumed that the debate over border security and immigration was in their own hands. And while Chicano rights organizations and employer lobbyists were often vehement in their efforts to keep the border open, illegal aliens themselves used to be mostly quiet about matters of immigration law. But in the spring of 2006, Americans witnessed millions of illegal aliens who not only were unapologetic about their unlawful status, but were demanding that their hosts accommodate their own political desiderata, from driver's licenses to full amnesty. Holding the largest demonstration on May Day, with thousands of protestors waving Mexican flags and bearing placards of the communist insurrectionist Che Guevara, only confirmed to most Americans that illegal immigration was out of control and becoming politicized along the lines of Latin American radicalism. In *Mexifornia*, I pointed to the incongruity of angry protestors waving the flag of the country they emphatically did not wish to return to, but now these images were beamed to millions on the evening news. The radical socialism of Latin America—reflected in the angry millions who flocked to Venezuela's Hugo Chavez, Bolivia's Evo Morales and Andrés López Obrador of Mexico—had now seemingly been imported into our largest cities.

Turmoil in areas of Mexico where many illegal aliens come from is especially worrisome. Recently, for example, nearly the entire state of Oaxaca was close to open revolt over efforts to force the resignation of the provincial governor Ulises Ruiz—with teacher rebellion, widespread lawlessness, vigilantism, and a complete breakdown of order. This turbulence in Mexico adds to the perception that illegal aliens increasingly arrive not merely as economic refugees, but as political dissidents who take to the streets to demand social justice, as was their custom back home. More importantly, Oaxaca's troubles cast doubt on the old conventional wisdom that illegal immigration is a safety valve that allows Mexico City critical time to get its house in order. Perhaps the opposite is true: some of the areas that send the most illegal aliens to the United States still experience the greatest social tensions—in part because of familial disruption and social chaos when adult males flee and depopulated communities in consequence become dependent on foreign cash.

Worker remittances sent back to Mexico from the United States now bring in about $15 billion annually in precious American dollars—equivalent to the revenue from 500,000 barrels a day of exported oil. Mexico cannot afford to lose its second-largest source of hard currency, and will do almost anything to ensure its continuance. The attitude of the Mexican government is another factor that has convinced many Americans that the border must be closed. When Mexico City publishes cartoons advising its own citizens how best to cross the Rio Grande, Americans are appalled. Not only does Mexico brazenly undermine American law in order to subsidize its own failures, but it also assumes that those who flee northward are among its least educated citizens, without much ability to read beyond the comic book level.

We are also learning that Mexico—beyond wanting its expatriates' cash or their lobbying efforts for Mexican interests once they are safely across the border—has little concern about the welfare of its citizens abroad in America, who live in crowded apartments, drive dangerous vehicles, and count on generous American health care and food subsidies while they send nearly half their modest wages back to the motherland. Thus Mexico exports its own citizens in the expectation that they will remain like serfs, surrendering much of the fruit of their toil to their distant masters.

Even more grotesquely, the real estate market in Baja California has been booming in the last five years. Once Mexico grasped that its own unspoiled coast was highly desirable to wealthy Americans as an extension of the prized but crowded Santa Barbara–San Diego seaside corridor, it began to reform its property and title law, and to welcome cash-laden expatriates with open arms. All this is sound economics, but with a dubious ethical message: Mexico City sends the United States millions of its own illiterate poor, whom it will neither feed nor provide with even modest housing, but at the same time invites in thousands of Americans with cash to build expansive second homes on choice seaside property.

Of course, the ultimate solution to the illegal immigration predicament is to bring Mexican society up to near the level of affluence found in the United States by embracing market reforms of the sort we have seen implemented in South Korea, Taiwan and China. But opponents of globalization do not see the proliferation of Wal-Mart superstores and Starbucks cafes down south in such terms. Rather, they wonder why Americans should get mad about Mexican illegals coming north when our own crass culture with its glaring English neon spreads southward. Such an argument neglects to mention that Americanization in Mexico occurs legally and brings capital, while Mexicanization in America occurs through illegal means and is driven by poverty.

The consequences of illegal immigration also reach the second generation, in which illegitimacy, high-school dropout rates and criminal activity have risen to such levels that no longer can we simply dismiss the situation as a replay of the problematic but eventually successful Italian immigration of the late nineteenth century. Since 1990, the number of poor Mexican-Americans has climbed 52 percent, a figure that has skewed overall U.S. poverty rates. Billions of dollars spent on our own poor are less likely to show up as encouraging social statistics when a million of the world's poor enter the country each year. While the number of impoverished black children has dropped 17 percent in the last sixteen years, the number of Hispanic poor has gone up 43 percent.

Illegitimacy rates are higher in Mexico than in the United States, but the force multiplier of illegal status, a language barrier and a lack of higher education means that second-generation Mexican-Americans suffer from illegitimacy rates higher than those found either in Mexico or in the United States generally. Currently, half of all births to Hispanics of all statuses are illegitimate—which is 42 percent higher than the illegitimacy rate for the American population as a whole.

Education levels reveal the same dismal pattern: nearly half of all Hispanics are not graduating from high school in four years. And the more Hispanic a school district becomes, the greater the rate of failure for Hispanic students. In the Los Angeles Unified School District, which is 73 percent Hispanic, 60 percent of all students are not graduating. But the real tragedy is that among those Hispanics who do graduate, only about one in five will have completed a curriculum that qualifies for college enrollment. That is why at many campuses of the California State University system, almost half the incoming class each year must take remedial courses. I found that teaching Latin to first-generation Mexican-Americans and illegal aliens was valuable not so much as an introduction to the ancient world, but as the student's first experience with remedial English grammar.

Less than 10 percent of those who identify themselves as Hispanic nationwide have graduated from college with a bachelor's degree. Meanwhile, almost one in three Mexican-American males age 18–24 in California, in response to a recent poll, reported having been arrested, and one in five has been jailed. Currently there are 15,000 illegal aliens in the California penal system.

Statistics like these have changed the debate radically. While politicians and academics assured the public that illegal aliens came only to work and would quickly assume an American identity, the public was seeing vast problems with crime, illiteracy and illegitimacy; and these observations have been borne out by hard data. In *Mexifornia* I related incidents of break-ins at my home, and of drivers crashing into our vineyards without licenses, registration or insurance; such incidents have continued in my own experience since the book appeared. But more importantly, anecdotal stories like these are now commonplace in the American Southwest. They are still ignored by elites or ridiculed as prejudicial, but the anecdotes are now supported by statistical studies.

The growing national furor over illegal immigration is apparent not only in the rightward shift of the debate, but also in the absence of any new arguments for open borders. In this climate of opinion, I welcome a new paperback edition of *Mexifornia*, with its theme that reasonable people must act forcefully and lawfully now before the present tragedy evolves into a catastrophe. Such a warning that time and reason are growing scarce seems more critical now than when it was first offered four years ago.

Preface

 I MET SANTIAGO LARA over twenty years ago. On a late March morning in 1982 he pulled into the orchard, jumped out of a broken-down station wagon filled with seven kids, caught me on the tractor and asked whether he could thin some plums until he found a new job. I had no idea who he was or where he came from. He looked exhausted—red-eyed, unshaven, in dirty clothes. I gave him what work I had, a temporary job for two days. Two decades later I still see him occasionally, and he still doesn't look good. Now over sixty, with white rather than raven-black hair, he continues as an occasional farm laborer and walks permanently stooped. He neither speaks a word of English nor has a single child who graduated from high school, although he has many children and grandchildren, some on various forms of disability, welfare and unemployment, others successful and gainfully employed, and a few who have been jailed.

When he left Mexico years ago his government wanted citizens like Santiago gone lest he agitate over his poverty or the bleak future looming for his children. In turn, he and millions like him were welcomed by Americans who wanted such immigrants to work cheaply for them. Liberals and ethnic activists wanted Santiago too, either as a future "progressive" voter or as another statistic in their loyal ranks of needy constituents. The rest of us didn't much care whether he came or stayed—as long as the economy remained strong and he avoided welfare and ensured that his kids graduated from high school. In fact Santiago, though he worked very hard, did neither.

Santiago Lara professes that he will die in Mexico, but there is something about the United States—or at least the mostly Mexican United States in which he lives—that makes even a visit home across the border almost unnecessary. We Americans, for our part, are unsure whether we want more, fewer, or no such Santiagos inside our borders, because we are confused over exactly what we are becoming. People from the rest of the country look at the eerie, fascinating thing that California is becoming, and they wonder about their own destiny.

I once thought Santiago and his children were going to become like us, but now I am not so sure. Instead, I think our state is becoming more like the Laras—or at least like something in between. In my small hometown of Selma in the middle of California's Central Valley, more people now speak Santiago's language than my own. The city's schools are more segregated than when I attended them forty years ago and their scholastic achievement is far lower. There are now more overt signs of material wealth among Selmans—new cars, cell phones, CD players, VCRs, color televisions—but also much more anger that "aliens," even if their fortunes have greatly improved in the United States, remain still poorer than the native-born. At the corner store there are more signs in Spanish than in English. And the government-subsidized apartment building two miles away is full of small children, baby carriages and young pregnant women—all evidence that someone at least still thinks big families are good in a world where many childless natives deem them bad.

So are we now a Mexifornia, Calexico, Aztlán, El Norte, Alta California, or just plain California with new faces and the same old customs? Many of us think about this in the abstract. Charles Truxillo, a Chicano studies professor at the University of New Mexico, for example, promises that some day we will all be part of a new sovereign Hispanic nation called "Republica del Norte" encompassing the entire Southwest. "An inevitability," Truxillo calls it, and it will obtain its sovereignty, he warns, "by any means necessary" as "our birthright."

What is the nature of California, traditionally the early warning sign to the rest of the nation, and what will be its eventual state of being? After September 11, 2001, the question of secure borders and a unified citizenry no longer stands afar in the future or remains a parlor game of academics and intellectuals, but is a matter of everyone's concern right now, both in and out of California. In a nation beset with new enemies who wish to destroy us, do we have common values and ideas that unite more than divide us? If our fundamentalist adversaries see us Americans of all colors, ethnicities and religions, without exception, as infidels deserving of death simply by virtue of being Americans, do we likewise see ourselves as a united people?

Is America, as our medieval foes assert, a single culture? Or are we, as many of our sophisticated, homegrown social critics allege, many cultures of many races? If snipers, suicide bombers and poisoners wish to kill indiscriminately black, brown, yellow and white Americans because they are alike, why do many professors, journalists and politicians claim that we are, and *should be*, different and separate? And in a world of sectarian killing—in Bosnia, Rwanda, Northern Ireland, India—is it wisdom or folly to emphasize our differences over our similarities, to champion separatism as preferable to assimilation, and toy with the principle that the law matters only according to the ephemeral circumstances and particular interests involved?

Our immigration dilemma is a simple but apparently unsolvable calculus: Americans want the work they won't do to be done cheaply by foreigners who, they wrongly assume, will inevitably transform themselves into Americans. In turn, the downtrodden Mexicans who come here and their elite advocates in America romanticize Mexico, a nation that brought them the misery they fled, while too often deprecating the place that alone gave them sanctuary. Everyone sees this—at least in the abstract—and can probably agree on the appropriate remedy: far less illegal immigration and a more measured policy of legal immigration, along with a stronger mandate for assimilation. But caught in a paralysis of timidity and dishonesty, we still cannot enact the necessary plans for a workable solution. To do so, after all, entails confronting a truth that is painful and might displease thousands who have grown comfortable with the present chaos. Who wants to be called an isolationist or a nativist by the corporate Right, and a racist or a bigot by the multicultural Left?

Mexifornia is about the nature of a new California and what it means for America—a reflection upon the strange society that is emerging as the result of a demographic and cultural revolution like no other in our times. Although I quote statistics gleaned from the U.S. Census and scholarly books on Mexican immigration into the United States, this is not an academic study with the usual extensive documentation. I write instead of what I have seen and heard living half a century in California's Central Valley, at the epicenter of the upheaval. Most of the children I went to school with were Mexicans or Mexican-Americans. Many of them remain my close friends today—inasmuch as I live on the same small farm south of Fresno where I grew up, 130 years after my great-great-grandmother built our present home. Those who speak of an explosion of illegal immigration into California usually cite the counties of Fresno, Kings and Tulare surrounding me and the nearby towns of Selma, Dinuba, Sanger, Parlier, Orange Cove, Cutler and Reedley as examples of California's radically changing demography and its attendant social and economic challenges.

For those of you who live outside of California, far away from Mexico, and sigh that the problem is ours, not yours: be careful. California has always been an idea, not merely a place. Our climate, social volatility and an absence of anything farther west always put us on the cutting edge. After all, we gave America Hollywood and with it the tabloid popular culture that rules our contemporary worldview. The modern protest movement began in

Berkeley. Gay rights called San Francisco home. Theme parks were born in southern California. Bikinis, bare navels, the dyed-blond look—they all showed up here first.

Wherever you live, if you want your dirty work done cheaply by someone else, you will welcome illegal aliens, as we did. And if you become puzzled later over how to deal with the consequent problems of assimilation, you will also look to California and follow what we have done, slowly walking the path that leads to Mexisota, Utexico, Mexizona or even Mexichusetts—a place that is not quite Mexico and not quite America either.

Many see a poetic justice in all this, a nemesis at work that clears the ledger of past transgressions. That at least is the attitude of many Hispanic activists. I have read dozens of their Chicano memoirs and scholarly studies that offer a vast compendium of racism and white prejudice. I offer the following recollection not to deny that such pathologies existed and were hurtful, but to suggest that the story was, and is, far more complex and not nearly so one-sided as they think. For every two ethnic slurs, there was an instance of enlightened kindness; for every bigoted teacher, there was someone who went out of her way to help illegal aliens; for every purportedly grasping corporate mogul, there were small farmers of Japanese, Armenian or western European background who worked alongside their laborers. And as someone who for the first six grades of school found himself part of a very tiny minority of rural whites at predominantly Mexican-American Jefferson and Eric White Schools on the west side of Selma, California, I remember ethnic tensions as being typically spawned by weak people of all backgrounds, rather than a comfortably familiar melodrama of predictable racial heroes and villains.

The people who jumped me as an eight-year-old from the blind side were often Mexican. Those who threatened to knife me at fourteen for no reason other than because I was white were Mexican. And the three youths who tried to break into my home and assault my family when I was forty were all Mexicans. But then so were all the friends who helped me fight back in grade school;

who have lived on our farm for forty years; and who as sheriffs and police come out to protect us today when there are problems.

I have been upset that drivers who have ruined my vineyard were illegal aliens with false identification. But then I also suspect that the immigration certificates of those who have harvested our grapes at the eleventh hour, when no one else would, were counterfeit as well. Immigration, assimilation and the entire dilemma of the Mexican border are insidious problems—a moral quagmire in which any posing as ethical instructors had better take care that they themselves, either implicitly or overtly, do not in some way benefit from the presence of unassimilated illegal aliens.

In some sense, I know Mexican-Americans perhaps better than I do so-called whites. I confess—not out of any racialist feeling, but simply because of habit and custom—that I feel more comfortable with the people I grew up with, a population of mostly Mexicans, Mexican-Americans, and whites who were raised with nonwhites. I have Mexican-American nephews, nieces, sisters-in-law and prospective sons-in-law as well as neighbors. My older brother married a Mexican-American; my twin brother married a high school friend who was divorced from a Mexican illegal alien. I married someone from Selma High School whose family had left Oklahoma during the Dust Bowl depression. The neighboring farmhouse to the west is home to resident Mexicans; so is the one immediately to the east. My two daughters are going steady with Mexican-Americans who grew up nearby in Selma; and the people I eat lunch with, talk with and work with are all either Mexican or Mexican-American. And so I have come to the point where the question of race per se has become as superficial and unimportant in my personal life as it has become fractious and acrimonious on the community, state and national levels. Some of the paradoxes, hypocrisies and hilarities that characterize California as a result of changing attitudes and more immigrants are subjects of this book.

Two themes dominate most of what has been written about Mexicans in California, and I have tried to avoid both. On the one extreme, we hear scary statistics that "prove" California will become part of Mexico by the sheer fact of immigration. On the other, we are told that either nothing much is changing, or that what alterations are occurring in the fabric of our social life are all positive. The truth, as always, is in between: California is passing through tumultuous times, but there is no reason to anticipate that it must become a de facto colony of Mexico. More importantly, I do not believe all that much in historical determinism—the idea that broad social, cultural and economic factors make the future course of events inevitable and render what individuals do in the here and now more or less irrelevant.

My main argument instead is that the future of the state—and the nation too, as regards the matter of immigration—is entirely in the hands of its current residents. California will become exactly what its people in the present generation choose to make it. So it is high time for honest discussion, without fear of recrimination and intimidation. How else are we ever going to sort out the various choices that will decide our collective fate—especially at a perilous time when we find ourselves at war with those who kill us as Americans regardless of accent, skin color or origin? That many in the business community will consider what follows naïve or dub me a protectionist/isolationist worries me as little as the critical voices I am sure to hear from an academic elite whose capital remains largely separatist identities and self-interest. Both parties, after all, did their part to get us into this predicament and have so far escaped accountability for the harm they have done.

I have changed the names of my teachers and associates in my hometown out of concern for their privacy, and because we live and work together. In three cases, to protect the identity of close friends I have made slight changes in the description of where they live and work. I thank my wife, Cara, and my colleague in classics at California State University, Fresno, Professor Bruce S. Thornton, another rural San Joaquin Valley native, for reading the manuscript and offering criticism and help. Peter Collier first suggested that I write the present book—an expanded version of an essay that appeared in *City Journal*. I thank him and also Myron Magnet, editor of *City Journal*, for help in editing both the present book and the original article. My literary agents, Glen Hartley and Lynn Chu, as always, have proven valuable representatives and friends.

Introduction

I WRITE HERE FROM THE PERSPECTIVE of a farmer whose social world has changed so radically, so quickly that it no longer exists. Three decades ago my hometown of Selma was still a sleepy little town in central California, halfway between Los Angeles and San Francisco, between the coast and the high Sierra. It was a close-knit community of seven thousand or so mostly hardscrabble agrarians whose parents or grandparents had once immigrated from Denmark, Sweden, Armenia, Japan, India, Mexico and almost every other country in the world, to farm some of the richest soil in the world. Selma's economy used to be sustained by agriculture—in the glory years before the advent of low prices caused by globalization, vertically integrated corporations and highly productive high-tech agribusiness—and supplemented by commuters who worked in nearby Fresno. The air was clear enough that you could see the lower Sierra Nevada, forty miles away, about half the year on average, not a mere four or five days following a big storm, as is now the case.

Sociologists call a small, cohesive town like the old Selma a "face-to-face community." As a small boy I used to dread being stopped and greeted by ten or so nosy Selmans every time I entered town. Now I wish I actually knew *someone* among the many I see.

The offspring of Selma's immigrant farmers learned English, they intermarried, and within a generation they knew nothing of the old country and little of the old language. Now Selma is an edge city on the freeway of somewhere near twenty thousand anonymous souls, and is expanding at an unchecked pace, almost entirely because of massive and mostly illegal immigration from a single country: Mexico. Because my great-great-grandmother arrived to carve out our present farm from desert in the 1870s, before Selma existed, and my children are the sixth successive generation to live in the house that she built, I was deeply attached to the old town, now vanished. It was by no means perfect, but it was a society of laws and customs, not a frontier town like the current one, in which thousands reside illegally, have no lawful documentation, and assume that Selma must adapt to their ways, not the reverse.

Time passes; things must change. And so I accept transformations that are inevitable: a price-cutting Wal-Mart would drive out our third-generation Japanese-owned nursery, and multinational agribusiness would overwhelm the once prosperous Sikh family farm down the road. While I saw all this happening as if by time lapse, I hoped that the new Selma would at least retain the language, customs, laws and multiracial but unicultural flavor of the old. But it has not.

I look at these things, however, also as a classics professor at the local California State University campus twenty-five miles away. As a historian I accept in the abstract that culture is unstable and always evolves—often radically. The Greek polis became the Hellenistic municipality; the Italian republic turned into the polyglot Roman Empire; Hebrew Palestine became in turns Persian, Greek, Roman, Arab, Ottoman, English and Israeli. By training, we in the academy are detached observers who try to inculcate a sense of distance and objectivity, an acceptance of the fact that history is restless and culture mutable. There are age-old processes far larger than ourselves, which predate us and will go on long after we are dead. So I mostly watch Selma and listen, trying to forget about my own past and present, and attempt to chronicle dispassionately what is going on around me—especially the strange paradox of immigrants streaming toward Western countries even as many are angry at themselves for doing so. I still try to drive out the echoes of my grandfather's subjective folk wisdom and my long-dead aunt's exhaustive Selma genealogies (e.g., "The youngest Josephson girl married Aram Eknonian's older brother who lived on Tucker Street") to replace it with the cold logic of Thucydides, who knew so well the nature of man and the predictable mess he creates (e.g., "an exact knowledge of the past [is] an aid to the understanding of the future which in the course of human things must resemble if it does not reflect it").

But immigration concerns me in yet another way: not just as a native or as a historian, but also as a teacher whose students increasingly come mostly from Mexico. For two decades I have driven up daily to the college campus at Fresno to teach persons, not "peoples," and so have seen that assimilation is still possible during the current immigration onslaught—if we forget group causes and the rhetoric of the multicultural industry, and simply concentrate on providing interested students with opportunities that match their often ignored aptitudes.

Mentors tend to claim primacy for their own disciplines—physicists swear that science will alone save us; educationists know that the nature of man is subject to improvement given the right pedagogical method; classicists insist that knowledge of philology, history and literature produces a singularly educated citizen. As one who teaches Latin and Greek to classes including many immigrants from Mexico, I have observed remarkable transformations in these immigrants that were as wonderful to me as they may have been problematic to many of my more "progressive" colleagues in the social sciences. Illegal aliens and Mexican residents who learned Latin, who came to speak perfect English, who were intimate with Roman consuls and the tragedy of Antigone tended to become proud American-Mexicans rather than unsure and troubled Mexicans, finding self-esteem in accomplishment rather than in therapeutic rhetoric. (I'm sure that the same is true for those who mastered quantum mechanics and any of the other solid disciplines.) Arturo, Gil, Jorge, Frank, Hortensia and dozens of others—the more they read Cicero and explored the beauty and paradoxes of Western civilization, the more they became prized and recruited candidates for graduate school, federal employment and corporate jobs—and the more often they told me about how their self-appointed ethnic caretakers in the university became disturbed at their evolution into something quite beyond the need for paternalistic counsel.

Arturo crossed the border illegally and after four years of college he reads Greek, Latin, French and German. Gil now runs a Latin class at the local junior high school. Jorge, who in Latin composition classes used to correct my own lectures on tenses of the subjunctive in subordinate clauses, is better educated than many of his professors at Cal State Fresno. Frank, a scholar of the early Church, left our MA program in ancient history to become a computer programmer. Hortensia wasn't sure exactly how four years of Greek and Latin could support her, but is now an exceptional primary school teacher. As far as I can tell years after their graduation, these young men and women left the university to take up productive professional lives while defining themselves as individuals and as Americans, rather than as part of a collective and dependent Mexican underclass.

Because of the disparate angles of my perception, this book is part melancholy remembrance of a world gone by, part detached analysis by a historian who knows well the treacherous sirens of romance and nostalgia, and part advocacy by a teacher who always wanted his students to be second to no one.

Thousands arrive illegally from Mexico into California each year. Indeed, our state is now home to 40 percent of America's immigrants. Such immigration from the south is hardly a new development along the porous 2,000-mile border between the United States and Mexico. For over a hundred years, Mexicans have easily fled into California and the wider American Southwest. Drought, political revolution and economic depression have all brought the desperate and oppressed in. Sometimes America's own recessions and backlashes have driven them back out. Yet something has changed since 1970—and changed profoundly.

True, the two decades of Mexican revolution between 1910 and 1930 gave us one million new arrivals, and subsequently the rate has often been nearly fifty thousand per year. What is *new* is not so much the increased volume of immigration, but a growing despair and uncertainty over how—or even whether—to assimilate the arrivals into the fabric of the United States. In America's immigration dilemma, no state is more unsure of itself (or more broke) than California—and perhaps for just that reason no home is more sought out by illegal aliens.

Most arrivals are given work by grateful employers. Indeed, businesses profit greatly from the aliens' much-needed labor—even as the audacious newcomers are increasingly resented by millions of other Californians for coming in such numbers and under such unlawful circumstances. Although illegal aliens are eager to get a fighting chance to succeed in America, many are not prepped for, nor immersed into the cutthroat competitive culture they help to mobilize.

Instead, in recent years they and their offspring have ended up in ethnic enclaves of the mind and barrios of the flesh. In these locations they often soon become dependent on subsidies—and too many of their children will join an underclass to be led by ethnic shepherds who often do more harm than good, however much they wish to help.

Since roughly 1970, the evolving concept of multicultural-ism—which holds that Western civilization merits no special consideration inasmuch as all cultures are of equal merit—has proved to be the force-multiplier of illegal immigration from Mexico. It turns a stubborn problem of assimilation into a social tragedy stretching across generations. Almost every well-intended and enlightened gesture designed to help immigrants in the last three decades—de facto open borders, bilingual education, new state welfare programs, the affirmation of a hyphenated identity, a sweeping revisionism in southwestern American history—has either failed to ensure economic parity or thwarted the processes of assimilation. Almost everything stern and uncompromising that for two centuries has helped other immigrants to the United States—language immersion, autonomy from government assistance, rapid assumption of an American identity, and eager acceptance of mainstream American culture—has either been discounted as passé or embraced only halfheartedly.

The backward-looking new ideology about Mexican immigration is obsessed with the racial prejudice and economic exploitation of the past—a wound repeatedly scrutinized by comfortable elites, but clearly not much of a hindrance to the millions of impoverished Mexicans and Indians who still risk their lives daily to reach the promised land of America, apparently glad to escape the wretchedness of their native land.

When ethnic chauvinism is preached by our elites (who often do not really practice it themselves), it creates situations with real consequences. Brothers with Mexican surnames get scholarships, while their half-siblings with equivalent records but non-Latino names do not. Friends of four decades suddenly drift apart because one is made to feel that his commitment to assimilation is somehow retrograde or proof of false consciousness. Our sense of history, both national and familial, is stolen from us—a longsuffering grandmother born in 1890 who worked hard is no longer remembered as a unique individual, but is categorized along with millions of anonymous others as simply an agent of past oppression.

Most Californians of all backgrounds understand these growing social and cultural costs that ultimately originate from their dependence on seemingly limitless cheap labor—the Devil's bargain we have made to avoid cutting our own lawns, watching our own kids, picking our peaches, laying our tile and cleaning our toilets. But despite the benefits that flow from the bargain, they are still ill at ease for having made it, although, because of fears that they will be disparaged as illiberal, they seldom voice openly what they feel. This situation led to successful ballot initiatives that cut off aid to illegals, ended affirmative action and curtailed bilingual education. And in the depressing circularity of the immigration dilemma, these referenda made sure that the subject was even more repressed—the third rail of California politics. It is often a war between street protest and simmering anger in the voting booth. Mexicans march to demand that Fresno's century-old and historic Kings Canyon Avenue—with a direct view of the majestic peaks—instantaneously become "Caesar Chavez Avenue." In response, furious Anglo voters make anonymous calls to talk shows and promise revenge in November. The Mexican-American caucus in the legislature demands that state universities, by fiat, graduate Hispanics at rates commensurate with the surrounding community's racial makeup—even as the electorate usually turns out in droves when such hot-button issues can be addressed behind a curtain with a faceless voting stylus.

Even timorous attempts to initiate an honest public discussion of the issue can earn one the cheap slander of "racist." Given the demagoguery of our elected state representatives and the general hostility to frank talk, it's no wonder that ballot propositions, led by unelected partisans and enacted through popular vote, are the preferred mechanism for ventilating the growing discontent. Embittered Californians decline to challenge the therapeutic bromides offered to Hispanics in their schools and state agencies —but then go quietly to the polls to vent their rage by ending what they see as special concessions to those who broke the law in coming here. It is not a very healthy state of affairs to have a voting population of millions thinking privately what they would never express publicly.

Confusion and disagreement abound even within families. I ask my brother whether he knows the true social costs generated by his plum-picking crew; he barks back, "Go to the mall, then, and get me some of those hardworking American teenagers." At our family Christmas dinner, a teenager who doesn't speak Spanish but gets government largess for being half "Hispanic" challenges me: "How do you know I won't experience prejudice later on because I have a Mexican name?" At various times we all contend over whether porous borders are California's hope, its certain bane, or again something in between.

And why should such uncertainty not arise, when even sup- posedly objective data cannot supplant private anecdote and personal bias? Liberal economists, for example, swear that legal immigrants to America bring in $25 billion in net revenue per annum. Yet more skeptical statisticians employing different models reach the radically different conclusion that aliens cost the United States over $40 billion a year, and that here in California each ille- gal immigrant will take from the state $50,000 more in services than he will contribute in taxes during his lifetime.

Some studies suggest that the average California household must contribute at least $1,200 each year to subsidize the deficit between what immigrants cost in services and pay in taxes— almost the price of a year's tuition at the California State University. More frequently, salaried taxpayers hector their legisla- tors about how they are paying in a myriad of insidious ways for the illegality practiced by contractors, farmers and factory owners. No wonder that we are simply confused and awash in a sea of con- tradiction: statisticians claim that we as a people find prices marked down by less than 1 percent as a result of illegal alien labor; but when it is proposed that we close or tighten our bor- ders, thousands of employers nevertheless forecast catastrophe and skyrocketing prices. We are told that blanket amnesty and legal sta- tus will ensure assimilation and prosperity; but statistics reveal that after twenty years, Mexican immigrants who have obtained lawful papers still have double the welfare rate of American citizens.

Meanwhile, illegal immigration from Mexico just continues on unabated. I think it always will because it unites the power and influence of employers with the rhetoric and threats of the race industry—a potent alliance that exercises its clout well beyond the actual numbers of the state's businessmen, social welfare bureaucrats, Chicano studies professors and La Raza activists. Right and Left, working in an uneasy partnership that trumps traditional political affinities, lobby for open borders to allow millions to come north. The *Wall Street Journal* and Chicano studies departments often agree on open borders, even as reactionary Pat Buchanan and ultraliberal Marin County yuppies conclude that enough is enough.

Unlike the Poles, Germans, Chinese, Greeks, Italians, Jews and Japanese, who usually came en masse and then stopped abruptly, Mexican immigration, at least since 1970, has proven to be a steady surf rather than a single tidal wave. Half of all legal immigrants to the United States come from Mexico. Three million were admitted legally into the country in the decade between 1986 and 1996. But no one has an accurate idea of how many arrived *illegally*. So sensitive is the issue that Californians cannot obtain reliable data on how many of its more than 10 million Hispanic residents have arrived here from Mexico unlawfully in the last two decades. Is it 2 million, 4 million, 6 million? Whatever the figure, the total number of residents of Mexican heritage has increased tenfold in the last thirty years. But even that figure is problematic because of the invisibility caused by intermarriage, the inability to count illegal alien populations, and the tendency of many Hispanics to list themselves as "white" on surveys rather than check the box that makes them officially a "person of color."

No one believes any longer the government's old insistence on a mere 6 million illegal residents nationwide. The figure may in fact be closer to somewhere between 8 and 12 million. Each year over 1.5 million aliens are apprehended attempting to enter the United States illegally, the vast majority on the southern border of the United States. Perhaps ten times that number are never caught. The U.S. Hispanic population—of which over 70 percent are from Mexico—grew 53 percent during the 1980s, and then between 1990 and 1996 rose another 27 percent. At present rates of birth and immigration, by 2050 there will be 97 million Hispanics who will constitute one-quarter of all Americans—and well over half the population of California!

Liberal Californians bristle at the suggestion that Hispanic families are larger than others, claiming that such a statement is racist or irrelevant since the children of assimilated upscale immigrants in time will surely show about the same fertility rates as non-Mexicans. That may be generally correct, yet as long as hundreds of thousands of illegals arrive unchecked every year, the state must continue to deal with a succession of first-generation immigrant families with three to six children at or below the poverty line. Moreover, no advocate in the university promotes family planning as a means of economic self-sufficiency; there is no campaign in Chicano studies departments encouraging immigrant families to have only one or two children so as to ensure financial solvency.

In contrast, most statisticians believe that population growth for non-Hispanics in California is flat or perhaps in decline, due to shrinking family size and emigration to other states. Without the yearly influx of large families by illegal immigration, the state population would reach a relative stasis in about ten or fifteen years. For decades, Californians were shrilly warned by liberals of a coming "population bomb" if they continued to have three and four children per family. Finally, the badgering took effect. Many of the affluent embraced the strange cultural ethic that large families were not only somehow undemocratic, but also took precious resources away from those who more wisely—or less egotistically—chose to limit their own progeny. In addition, the prosperity of the last three decades—unlike the good times of our agrarian past—did not encourage large families. Instead, affluence hooked both suburban parents on full-time employment to maintain an increasingly bountiful, but also tenuous consumer lifestyle, one felt to be impossible to sustain with more than one or two dependent children. In places like Menlo Park, Santa Rosa and Monterey there is an entire generation of childless married couples, thousands of gay households and many affluent professional singles who no longer see child-raising as either their social duty or integral to their own personal happiness.

Yet at the very time the new creed took hold across class lines that small families were economically wise, culturally desirable, socially progressive and the only way to ensure a choice few children full opportunity—everything from piano lessons at three years of age to SAT preparation at ten—California's population was exploding. It grew mostly from immigration, both legal and not, and involved the slow assimilation of first- and second-generation immigrants who, at least initially, shared few of the liberal assumptions about the necessity or the desirability of reducing family size. One of my liberal friends recently summed up his "dilemma" when he explained to me that he had sired one child to guarantee her the maximum of parental attention and financial support, yet he now was slowly realizing that she would live in a state where millions of her peers got neither much attention nor adequate support—a development as depressing to him as he felt it might someday be dangerous to his daughter.

A far greater moral problem looms a mere decade from now, when the aging white population of the Baby Boomer generation finally—and nearly all at once—reaches retirement. Influential, affluent, informed (and not shy about self-interest or self-promotion), it will demand that Social Security and state retirement programs continue to be funded at promised levels. But these benefits will remain possible only with a complacent majority population of younger Hispanics who have large families and often work for wages lower than what retired whites with no dependents will receive. It will be a strange thing to see the 1960s generation of California elites in their seventies on the golf course or at the coffeehouse, drawing Social Security in aggregate amounts greater than what they contributed, and using that annuity as pocket money to supplement their private retirements and savings—as long as the darker-skinned groundskeepers and waitresses nearby keep working to pay hundreds of dollars per month in deductions that might otherwise have gone to support their six or seven dependents. (The Social Security tax bite is mostly fixed across class lines, not calibrated by income levels to the same degree as the income tax.)

Cringing at the thought of these and similar contradictions, neither Republican nor Democratic leaders officially wish to discuss cross-border traffic honestly. Both are unsure of the volatile public mood on any given day—unsure whether Californians of all races will finally say *no mas*, or whether those who are part Mexican or married to Mexican-Americans will vent their wrath at the polls or slander them on the evening news. The two parties, for reasons of money and power, ignore the social chaos brought by millions of illegal aliens: capitalists count on profits from plentiful, cheap workers, while activists expect these laborers to become liberal voters. And no wonder: in the 1996 election, over 70 percent of all Hispanic voters opted for the Clinton-Gore ticket.

Yet the actual aggregate Mexican-American vote that the Democrats so eagerly court remains just a fraction of the eligible pool. For example, a few miles away from me in the small upscale town of Hanford, of the 14,173 residents who identified themselves as Latino (34 percent of the town's entire population), *only 770 are registered to vote.* And we have no idea how many of that 770 actually voted on election day last November. The Mexican-American liberal electorate may be a chimera that will never materialize because immigrants assimilate and grow more conservative—or it may be a huge bottled genie that promises unending political power to any who can one day release it.

Illustrating the law of unintended consequences, the present immigration crisis is not quite what any of the stakeholders anticipated. For in addition to some cheap labor, the tax-conscious Right also got thousands of unassimilated others who eventually plugged into the state's nearly bankrupt entitlement industry and filled its newly built prisons. (Almost one-quarter of California's inmates are from Mexico, and almost a third of recent drug-trafficking arrests involved illegal aliens.) In contrast, the pro-labor

Left, salivating over a larger bloc vote, slowly discovered that the wages of its own impoverished domestic constituencies were eroded by less expensive and more industrious alien workers (50 percent of real wage labor losses was recently attributed by the Labor Department to the influx of cheap immigrant labor)—and that puts a strain on the coalition that the Left wants to build.

It is hard for progressive unions to be eager for imported labor from Mexico when millions of second-generation Mexican-American and African-American laborers are making not much above the minimum wage. Indeed, one of the unforeseen results of the infamous "Operation Wetback" that sought to deport illegal immigrants during the 1950s was a rapid increase in wage labor for legal farm workers throughout the Southwest. Conversely, some studies indicate that the presence of plentiful foreign laborers in the 1990s reduced the wages of unskilled workers by 5 percent. So does tough border control unfairly exclude Mexican nationals from the American dream, or does it assure Mexican-American citizens that their labor will be fairly rewarded?

Perplexed liberals of northern California are in a special dilemma. Committed to a multicultural agenda that does not "privilege" any particular heritage and in theory favors granting the world's poor nearly unlimited access to America, they nevertheless are also keen environmentalists who adamantly support population control. A San Francisco Bay Area Sierra Club member with one or two children who drives a fuel-efficient Volvo or a small four-wheel-drive Toyota, loves to backpack and fights for the state's shrinking open spaces cannot help but be worried over news that California's population is destined to grow to 50 or 60 million souls in the next twenty years—almost all of that increase the result of either illegal immigration or the large families of first- and second-generation Hispanic newcomers. For example, in the two-year period between the 2000 Census and the end of 2002, California's population growth by 872,000 was almost entirely due to immigration, mostly from Mexico and much of it illegal. To go from trying to stay alive while crossing the border, to enjoying the bounty of Kmart and Burger King, to joining the Nature Conservancy and the Sierra Club is a complex task requiring more than a single generation.

What happens when all that assiduous effort to recycle trash, block power-plant construction and try to ban internal combustion engines butts up against the real needs of millions of the desperate who first want the warmth of four walls, a flush toilet and basic appliances? Tearing out vineyards in the Central Valley to build HUD-supported housing tracts ensures such immigrants a decent home. Erecting more freeways accommodates millions more of the second-hand, often severely polluting cars that poor immigrants drive. Building schools, hospitals and clinics meets the rising demands of millions of young Hispanics without birth control or insurance. And all these services are somewhat antithetical to preserving untamed whitewater rivers (which could be dammed to provide water and power for a thirsty, energy-hungry state), green belts (which cause the remaining usable land to become too expensive for affordable new tract houses), and stringent restrictions on dumping, hunting, fishing, camping and use of public lands (which mostly hurt the poor, who rarely are acquainted with complex laws or have easy access to proper public facilities).

Even the libertarians of California have their own dilemma. In theory, they advocate open borders—the Chicano dream of *sin fronteras*—and the idea that capital flow, not centralized government, adjudicates who comes and who goes. In principle, they support the right of a small businessman to choose who works for him—preferably for low pay and with little hassle. But in reality, the free-market and corporate establishment sighs when thousands of California residents root for Mexico to beat the United States in the World Cup. A contractor or a farmer going to his favorite restaurant is piqued to witness two dozen men, exhausted from work, stripped to their boxer shorts while their work clothes are in the wash at the laundry next door. And the motel owner who relies on just such immigrants as housekeepers does not like to keep seeing gang shootings on the nightly news, wrecked cars on the roadside, or her taxes going into new prisons. So like their Sierra Club counterparts, the politically independent mogul, the agribusinessman and the small entrepreneur are all rethinking the political orthodoxy that once committed them to open borders. With no consistent ideology, they are sometimes stunningly hypocritical in simultaneously hiring illegal aliens and advocating immigration reform.

Californians of all political shades are now carefully weighing the pros and cons of illegal immigration at current rates—the business establishment most of all. Wages to illegals are often paid in cash, which is a bargain for everyone involved. For instance, at $10 an hour without state, federal and payroll taxes deducted, the worker really earns the equivalent of a gross $13 an hour or more, while the employer saves over 30 percent in payroll contributions and expensive paperwork. Meanwhile, however, such cash payments force other Americans and legal immigrants to pay steeper taxes in part to cover those who pay none. So the farmer cheering over access to solid, dependable, cheap labor is now learning that he pays more than he thinks for illegal aliens in the form of rising taxes as well as a fraying social fabric.

Polls taken even before September 11, 2001, showed that over 70 percent of Americans wanted immigration reduced. Nearly 90 percent reported that they would insist on English as the official language of the United States. Recently this conversation has shifted markedly to the right, as topics that only two or three years ago would have resided outside mainstream discussion—sending American troops to the border or summarily deporting illegal residents—have become the stuff of evening news debates.

My once sleepy hometown of Selma, California, in the center of the San Joaquin Valley, is again in the middle of all this. The formerly rural community has grown from a few thousand to over twenty thousand in a mere three decades—as a result of immigration from Mexico, mostly illegal. On our streets I have no idea whether the mostly young male illegal aliens I meet are economic refugees or fugitives from crime in Mexico, perhaps serious felons—and no one else does either, because there is no legal record of their existence, and what documents they and our local authorities possess are almost always fraudulent, forged to mask the conditions of their arrival. In the 1950s Mexicans flocked to do agricultural labor in the surrounding orchards and vineyards, usually in manageable numbers and under legal auspices. But since 1970 the community has simply become a good place to find safe refuge from Mexico as well as all sorts of work—construction, hotels and restaurants, fabrication—in the bedroom communities that surround Fresno. Our social problems are hardly white on Mexican, but often Mexican-American on Mexican—or rather, the struggle by second- and third-generation Americans of Mexican ancestry who run our schools, police our streets and manage our city government to cope with thousands of break-ins yearly, vandalism, hit-and-run accidents, drug manufacture and distribution, and public schools and hospitals that are overflowing with clients who speak little English and have little capital, but expect instantaneous American-style service.

Selma is now somewhere between 60 and 90 percent Hispanic. But then how does the government count those who do not wish to be counted? Even *legal* immigrants from Mexico rarely become citizens: of all those admitted legally to the United States since 1982, only 20 percent had become citizens by 1997. Some local schools, like my former elementary campus two miles from our farm, are 95 percent first-generation Mexican immigrants. How many are U.S. citizens is either not known or not publicly disclosed.

At the gas station a mile away from our farm, I rarely hear English spoken. Almost every car of immigrants that pulls in displays a Mexican flag decal somewhere. In our local cemetery I try to put flowers on the graves of our dead, even as I tiptoe around pinwheels, streamers, tiny wooden crosses and the litter left from eating and drinking. The graveyard where everyone from my great-great-grandmother to my parents and sister and fifteen other kin are buried is no longer a staid and sometimes grim European-inspired field of memory, but a more raucous picnic ground to commemorate the days of the dead with talking and snacks. Yet as I pass families laughing and chatting, sitting on blankets around the headstones, they hassle me as little as I them. I think that we both silently pray that their children will prove as industrious as they have been. Periodic visits to the final resting place remind me that we are all united in California, at least in that we generally will not get out of here alive.

What are we to make of it all—illegal aliens' baffling failures and clear successes, immigration's explicit costs and implicit benefits? I think it best to imagine present-day California as a wild frontier, every bit as exciting, dangerous and feral as the Mother Lode gold towns circa 1849. Then prospectors also came for the promise of El Dorado—and likewise in numbers beyond the powers of the law and government to absorb. Just as it was not clear then whether early California would sink into chaos or emerge energized by its hardworking new arrivals, so too our own future is again in doubt.

California, after all, best summarizes the entire paradox of illegal immigration into the United States. It is the most liberal and affluent area of the Southwest, as well as America's largest and most forward-looking state. Our upscale lifestyle is famous for being easy, laid-back and nonjudgmental. In contrast, our new-comers are not the elite or even the middle class from a poorer country, but the most uneducated and destitute of the entire North American subcontinent—usually not those of Spanish heritage, but Indians fleeing discrimination and hatred.

What a potentially explosive mix this experiment has become, not only mingling races, cultures and classes, but also test-ing very concretely California's often abstract commitment to progressive ideas. Standing athwart Californians' path to their envisioned utopia of pristine redwoods, dot.coms and air-conditioned malls are millions of the world's poorest. And the state simply cannot quite figure out whether it has become a promised land based on cheap immigrant labor or a looming nightmare of unassimilated Third-Worldism.

ONE

What Is So Different
about Mexican Immigration?

 DESPITE ITS STATUE OF LIBERTY, recitations of Emma Lazarus's poetry, and melting-pot imagery, America has always struggled with issues of immigration—mostly when it was a matter of the poor, dispossessed non-Anglos or non-Protestants coming in by the millions. Boatloads of refugees were denied entrance to the United States during the Holocaust. Starving Irish were compared to lower primates and denied employment; Italians were demeaned as little more than criminals; Poles were dismissed as stupid menials fit only for unskilled labor. As for "Oriental" immigration, there is no need to talk of it, since whole university departments now exist to explore the racism of the "Yellow Peril."

North America was originally settled largely by northern Europeans—English, Germans, Scandinavians, French and Dutch—who came as farmers and settlers in the late seventeenth through the early nineteenth centuries and set the cultural protocols, so in effect they enjoyed a head start in adaptation, which later arrivals have not had. But even then, there was prejudice from an entrenched Anglo-Saxon elite; my grandfather's Swedish family came en masse to California to help found the town of Kingsburg (near Selma), the idea being that only within a colony of similar "stupid square-heads" could Swedes be left alone to prosper.

The second wave of immigrants—southern Europeans,

Asians, Irish and Latinos—encountered an entrenched dominant culture of mostly Anglo- and northern-European Protestants, and suffered accordingly. Entire libraries document the plight of these aggrieved arrivals and their strange century-long metamorphosis from the despised "other" into the accepted majority of "whites"—as their growing incomes slowly washed away their racial and religious differences.

In a narrow sense, the mass arrival of millions of poor Mexicans is not all that different from the great influx of other groups who were poor and not northern European. We see now some of the same evolutionary signs that appeared in the nineteenth century: one to two generations of poverty and frequent degradation, followed by a generation of middle-class Mexican-Americans intermarrying with other groups and moving into traditional suburbs. Between 1995 and 2000, Hispanic income on average grew 27 percent—a rate of growth faster than that of any other minority group—as a virtually new class of assimilated and affluent Mexican-Americans arose. Their culture was now indistinguishable from the majority culture, and thus their ethnicity was quickly redefined as more or less "white," as had happened to Greeks, Italians, Armenians and Punjabis before them.

Yet the old assimilationist model—still secretly admired, but publicly ridiculed—is working efficiently for only a minority of new immigrants, given their enormous numbers and the peculiar circumstances of immigration from Mexico in the last half-century. So what accounts for the stubborn resistance to assimilation, besides the increased numbers and our own lack of confidence in the melting pot? What makes Mexican immigrants so different even from the recently arrived Armenians, Chinese, Russians or Laotians?

Why, for example, do my second-generation Asian students often speak little Lao or Korean, date non-Asians, become hyper-American in their tastes and prejudices, and worry (often openly and rudely) about the sheer numbers of Mexican people who speak poor English, show few professional skills, and are overrepresented in our jails? And why do my Mexican-American students, even those of nearly 100 percent Indian heritage, face hostility from their own ethnic communities when they assimilate, speak perfect English, and prefer Latin and Greek literature to Chicano studies, attend the annual classics picnic but not the separate Latino graduation ceremony, and consider themselves about as Mexican as I see myself Swedish?

Proximity

The obvious explanation is the closeness of Mexico, only a short drive to the south rather than oceans away. You can leave Los Angeles and be across the border in about three hours. That geographical nearness—the fact that the richest economy in the world is but a stone's throw from one of the most backward—has always been unfortunate for the Mexican arrival. It is hard to dream of a society further removed from a Mexican ghetto or rural village than is a California suburb. Had Mexicans flocked to Costa Rica, or had New Zealanders rushed into Los Angeles, the present problems of both hosts and guests would be nonexistent. Instead, a young man leaves his pueblo in Yucatan where cattle are starving for lack of fodder, and in two or three days he is mowing, bagging and dumping fescue grass in the most leisured and affluent suburb in America.

Moreover, for the *campesino* from Mexico there is little physical amputation from the mother country. In contrast, most other arrivals to California found the trip here a psychological guillotine. Their motherland—the Philippines, China, Japan, Basque Spain, Armenia, the Punjab—was cut clean off and discarded. The traditional homesick immigrant was now barricaded in his new homeland by thousands of miles of ocean, with little hope of returning to the Old Country every few months, and thus had to deal with Americans. For the Mexican immigrant, by contrast, the Rio Grande is no ocean, but a trickle easily crossed by a drive over a tiny bridge. A limited visitation, a family reunion—but usually not a permanent return—nourished enough nostalgia for Mexico to war with the creation of a truly American identity.

Most earlier mass migrations were also largely one- or two-time affairs—explosive eruptions rather than a steady flow. The Irish came mainly in the decades after the great mid-nineteenth-century famines, but rarely arrive in any great numbers today. Jews once fled the pogroms of Russia and Eastern Europe, but no longer immigrate as whole communities. The Cubans came in the hundreds of thousands after the fall of Batista, but after a mere forty years living in their Little Havana they are becoming assimilated and Americanized. Some Floridians may complain that their state's culture resembles Cuba, but in fact because there have *not* been hundreds of thousands arriving yearly from Cuba, the expatriate Cuban community is doomed—albeit slowly and almost invisibly—to lose its language and culture.

There is also a reason why the white minority in Miami, unlike its equivalent in Los Angeles, is envious of Latinos, and that revolves around the community's undeniable commercial success—a phenomenon not entirely explained by the old generalization that "Cuban immigrants were middle-class refugees and Mexican newcomers were not." Instead, the astute Cuban-American must admit privately, "Thank God for the island of Cuba and for Castro himself, which barred the way back and cut us loose on our own here." Mexicans, on the other hand, migrate by simply walking across a porous border, steadily replenishing the Hispanic community in the United States with fresh aliens who strengthen ties with the world south of the border. Consequently, even after twenty years, 8 out of 10 never become naturalized American citizens—a statistic essentially impossible for expatriate Cubans who fled Castro's communism.

But again, the heart of the problem in California is always the truth we know versus the lie we speak. The reality is that, despite the grandiose boasts, the protestations of undying allegiance and the menacing outbursts of national pride, few immigrants ever really want to return to Mexico. Very few wish to live as they did in Mexico, to live with others who remain part of Mexico—in other words, to be a Mexican *in Mexico* rather than a Mexican in California. It is one thing to receive treatment and care from a Los Angeles oncologist and chemotherapist, quite another to endure a growing tumor in central Mexico. Professors of Chicano studies here fret about the loss of Spanish, the rising rates of intermarriage and the steady erosion of a "Chicano identity"; yet none wish to replenish their roots by moving their families to rural Mexico and a world of untreated sewage, parasite-infested water and herbalists standing in for cardiologists.

The more sober observers of all races know that if Mexico were separated from the border by a hundred miles of ocean, the so-called minority problem in California would vanish within a generation or two. As it now stands, the constant stream of new arrivals means that for each assimilated Mexican, there are always several more who are not. Unlike Southeast Asians, who came all at once to California and from thousands of miles away following the disaster in Vietnam, Mexicans have had no opportunity to mature together and slowly evolve as a distinct cohort into Americans.

In fact, the opposite is true. An Italian or a Jew knew that if he did not learn English and the American system, he was going to be left behind as his peers pressed ahead. A Mexican in California senses that if he fails to integrate into mainstream American society, there will always be thousands more newcomers like himself who will know almost nothing about the United States, and thus by sheer numbers join him in a viable expatriate culture. A Pole once accepted that she would perpetually stumble through the Cleveland phone book if she kept speaking Polish; a Mexican accepts as a given that Pacific Bell will double the size of its directory assistance just to accommodate her Spanish.

Race

Race—could it be any other way in contemporary America?—is often cited as the most critical issue blocking the aspirations of

Hispanics. The standard doctrine, promulgated by university ethnic studies departments, is well known: Mexicans were never able to morph as easily into "whites" as did the discriminated-against Jews or Irish simply because, like African-Americans, they were a people of a darker color and thus, throughout the long brutal history of the Southwest, were deemed inferior by the racist white majority. Indeed, who can deny the sometimes shameful exploits of the Texas Rangers or the visceral contempt that the great southwestern cattle barons had for the Mexican menial laborer whom he treated little better than his cows?

The problem with the accepted dogma is not that it is entirely false—thousands of racist writings and years of official biased protocol can indeed be used to substantiate such a view—but that it is only a *partial* explanation for Mexican disappointments, and in any case it belongs largely to the past. If only skin color can ensure entrée into American society, how have Arabs, Koreans, Armenians and Japanese found parity with, and in many cases economic superiority over, the traditional white majority? Jet-black Punjabis, for example, are prominent in the professions of central California—medicine, law, agribusiness and academia—oblivious to the fact that their hue is often darker than that of African-Americans. Asians have a higher per capita income than California whites.

Thus the challenge is not to identify racism, but *to assess the degree to which it or its legacy can affect a people today.* Punjabis historically have not always been treated nicely in America, but they come from thousands of miles across a wide ocean with identifiable skills, close family networks, some English proficiency, a willingness to learn more, and a tradition of entrepreneurship, all of which seem to make race irrelevant. In fact, their ebony children who attend elite universities are not eligible for affirmative action. If anything, the University of California subtly and off the record looks askance at their overrepresentation—and this is an institution that already has been publicly rebuked for using de facto quotas in turning away qualified Asians from its Berkeley campus.

Californians are increasingly cynical and sense that affirmative action and special preferences are based neither on skin color nor on patterns of past discrimination, but simply are tied clumsily to a particular minority's failure to match the perceived economic performance of whites.

Koreans, likewise, are as "unwhite" as Mexicans; yet their culture puts a premium on business, education and family, not government largess. Like the Punjabi immigrants of today, and like the Japanese, Chinese and Armenian immigrants of the past, they have shrugged off the worst sorts of racial prejudices. So far, Mexican-American citizens have not been interned; nor have they been blown to bits while building railroads; nor have they suffered a holocaust by an invading Islamic power—disasters that did not stop the Japanese, Chinese and Armenians from reaching per capita economic parity with the majority in California. These other immigrants were at the end of their migrant odysseys and more likely to ponder the present and the future than to live in the past. I suppose "Don't get mad, get even" was thematic among these other victims of American racism and oppression. In my hometown of Selma, Armenians were zoned out of particular neighborhoods in the 1920s and were refused entry to the municipal swimming pool. Yet in two generations their capital and influence ensured that their homes and their private pools were the town's largest and most envied.

No Armenian today, despite skin color with a higher melanin content than that of the average white, claims to be "a person of color." Most Japanese do not either. "A person of color" does not necessarily mean that someone is, in fact, "colored" in any real sense; the term is largely absent among communities of dark Punjabis, Arabs, Greeks, Armenians and a host of brown and olive peoples. Instead, the nomenclature advertises that the self-described minority has deliberately defined himself in opposition to whatever "white" culture is—either out of real pride, justified anger, petty hurt, racial hatred or simple crass opportunism. And in a state rapidly growing more multiracial, we will soon need racial rubrics like those of the old Confederacy, backed by new-age genetic tracking, to figure out who exactly is "a person of color"—one-third, one-half or one-sixteenth nonwhite blood?

In any case, money has always eventually trumped race in America. The truism that race matters above all is forgotten when people of color earn more or become better educated than white people, but it returns with a vengeance when they remain isolated, poor and dependent. For all our boutique hatred of the moneyed classes, we accept that American plutocracy is a far more fluid system of opportunity than entrenched European or Asian hierarchies of class, color, ancestry and education. In sum, that racism has been a factor in the Mexican experience is indisputable; that in the present world of integration, intermarriage and government subsidy it still largely explains the disappointment and failure of millions of aliens is false.

Mexico City

Few observers of the immigration fiasco wish to talk honestly about the complex nature of Mexican society and the interplay there between race and poverty. Forget that the country is as poor as India and as chaotic as Zimbabwe, and far closer to us than either. There is something about the Mexican government that lies at the heart of the immigration mess—especially its passive-aggressive attitude toward the United States and its intellectually dishonest approach to the immigration problem.

Overlook for a moment that Mexico has never had any real history of sustained legitimate government, and only recently has taken the first steps in creating a multiparty system with free elections, an independent judiciary and an open media. And that its professed worries about its own citizens coming north to be exploited by American agribusiness resulted in a transitory policy of containment that was never really enforced and was largely ignored. Instead, the key to understanding Mexico's perplexing attitude toward America is simply found in Thucydidean exegesis: it is a proud state that was invaded twice by the United States and defeated, losing a great amount of its own territory—land which then thrived due to *the very fact of its separation from Mexico.* Those realities are not forgotten by Mexico. Japan might be defeated and humiliated by the United States, have its citizens in America incarcerated, its leaders hung and jailed, and its entire culture altered by American fiat—and then build an economic powerhouse to compete with and rival its former conqueror, all without constant tutorials about the evils of Okinawa. But Mexico seeks salve for its self-inflicted wounds in the history of a century past, rather than embrace honestly its own failures in the present.

The Irish government perhaps once regretted, but still accepted that its population had to leave or starve. Eastern European states were glad to see the Jews go on their journey to America. These governments lost control of their immigrants the minute they arrived in the United States. Such is not the case with Mexico, which both deliberately exports its unwanted and, once they safely reach American soil, suddenly becomes their champion and absent parent, as much out of resentment toward the United States as in real concern for people whom they apparently are so gladly free of.

At the heart of the problem with Mexico are class, race, politics and economics. Simply put, Mexican elites rely on immigration northward as a means of avoiding domestic reform. Market capitalism, constitutional government, the creation of a middle-class ethic or an independent judiciary will never fully come to Mexico as long as its potential critics go north instead of marching for a redress of grievances on the suited bureaucrats in Mexico City.

Supporters of financial bailouts and unrestricted immigration perhaps err when they claim that such engagement is necessary to prevent a Mexican catastrophe. Unfortunately, the opposite is more likely to be true: there is *always* catastrophe in Mexico, and our complicity—in addition to protecting American investment in Mexico—postpones an evolution in Mexican society that could finally force a rapacious aristocracy to the table for needed concessions.

Reform and transparency in Mexico are stalled—understandably, since every day's delay means more flight by the oppressed, not progress for the beleaguered who remain behind. One can imagine the state of politics in America should the nation's unemployed, uninsured and insecure decide to walk across the border to Canada by the millions each year: our reactionaries would have little to fear from the less affluent who stay, and our reformers would have little constituency. (Liberal Canadians, who now preen about their generally open immigration policies, would quickly fortify their border if thousands of starving and illiterate Americans began to pour into Toronto or Montreal every month to receive Canadian entitlements.)

To restructure the economy of Mexico, democratize the political system and legalize the courts would be to empower the Indians of the rural and mountainous hinterland, and thereby keep millions of them home as a vocal force for further change, rather than push millions and their problems northward. "Safety valve" is an inadequate term to indicate how useful a mass outflow of the poorest is for the Mexican status quo. This, after all, is a society sitting on a demographic time bomb of almost 100 million with a population growth rate of 2 percent per annum—and no feasible way of providing jobs, health care, social justice or personal safety to a nation half of which will soon be under the age of twenty-five. Without the promised land to the north, there might well loom either political revolution or African-style famine and plague.

The Mexican government's rationale—can we not detect its pernicious legacy also here in California?—is that the Yanquis and gringos once invaded the country, stole the land and rigged the border to harm permanently the Mexican people, who, through no fault of their own, are now crowded into too little space and find themselves oppressed by *el Norte* and the evil Anglos. The legacy of autocracy, a corrupt legal system, tribalism, statism, endemic racism, poor education, an absence of family planning, the lack of religious diversity and a nationalism of bad faith are rarely mentioned in Mexicans' inventory of the causes for the massive pell-mell flight of its citizens northward.

No wonder the Mexican government so often slanders us, alleging unprovoked hostility in our rather pathetic attempts to plug the border with wire, steel and concrete as well as overworked and much-maligned border guards. Some pundits in Mexico City like to compare our feckless efforts at keeping Mexicans out to the Berlin Wall and other old communist partitions designed to keep citizens *in.* Yet walls historically bring a painful honesty to problems. They brutally define the nature and the direction of human traffic. Communist fortifications were an admission that people wanted out. A fenced Hong Kong, on the other hand, was proof that nobody was dying to reach Peking. The wall currently proposed by the Israelis is anathema rather than a godsend to Palestinians, who, it turns out, want the freedom to enter hated Israel for work, commerce and profit—and perhaps even to secure safe transit to Brooklyn—rather than cross into a kindred Lebanon or Jordan. Closer to home, our border barricades are a painful reminder that no American wants out, but millions of Mexicans most assuredly want *in* to the United States—a stark truth that cuts through almost all the nonsense about immigration and race that emanates from both sides of the border.

Other advantages surely accrue to the Mexican status quo from its leaders' deliberate export of their own citizenry in staggering numbers. Most obviously, billions of much-needed foreign dollars are sent back into Mexico from its quasi citizens up north, legal and otherwise. An enormous expatriate community in America (Los Angeles is one of the largest urban concentrations of Mexicans in the world) gives Mexico leverage in its relationship with the United States, which involves billion-dollar loan guarantees and the creation of free-trade leagues—along with the apparent freedom to follow Middle Eastern oil price hikes at will. Feigned concern over its poor abroad in the United States also provides the bureaucrats in Mexico City with some camouflage of compassion and commiseration in dealing with its skeptical and neglected underclass at home. I often see the Mexican consular official in Fresno on television, for example, lecturing Americans on how inconsiderate they are to Mexicans here illegally. To my knowledge, not one interviewer has ever asked the official *why* they are here and not there. A Mexican government official is rightly irate when an alien has been roughed up by a California sheriff, but wrongly silent when dozens of *campesinos* on the wrong side of the border are gunned down by the Mexican police.

So there has indeed been complicity on the part of Mexico in the great migration north. And there has been a shameful and unforgivable absence of honesty on the part of our own political and academic establishment in legitimizing Mexico's venality. The Mexican government looks on the exportation of its poorest Indians as an economic issue: remittances from illegal aliens reach the billions of dollars and so prop up the Mexican government and help feed the starving who otherwise would look in vain to a non-existent safety net at home.

There is also an element of racism involved—one oddly ignored in the race-charged debates in contemporary America. For the most part it is not light-skinned Mexicans of Spanish heritage who are coming to the United States, but rather the poorest and brownest, largely Indian—and this apparently suits an elite in Mexico City that does not wish to explain why the whiter people of Mexico are better off than those who are browner. Indeed, if one were studiously to watch any of the Spanish-language television stations—whether owned and operated by Mexican nationals or by Mexican-Americans—one would surmise that surely the Ku Klux Klan had a hand in the programming. Most are either white or coated with white pancake makeup; nearly every prominent woman is a dyed blonde; every privileged host and hostess is about as Anglo-looking as can be. Yet all the characters who are subservient—taxi drivers, maids, gardeners, "the help"—resemble the hundreds of thousands of darker-skinned people who risk their lives to enter the United States illegally.

I have met wealthy elites, academics and journalists from Mexico City who privately laugh that they are exporting their Indians and Mestizos, their unwanted, into the United States. Their smile disappears when I reply that we instead figure what they suppose to be riffraff are the real cream of Mexican society: frontiersmen and women whose endurance and courage are good prerequisites for Americanization, and who in fact are superior people to those who oppress them at home. So while the powers in Mexico City regard departure as good politics—a valve of sorts that releases dangerous pressures rather than allow explosions of the type that occurred in the country's earlier checkered history—in an odd way the joke ultimately is on them. Within twenty years the poor, brown Indian alien could enjoy a material existence in America superior to that of the upper-class white Mexican in Mexico City.

Reverse Chauvinism

There are also other themes that explain the Mexican government's peculiar rationale for sending millions of its own citizens out of the country. Surely an element of pique is involved. Mexico, whose vast natural resources of fertile land, oil and minerals have not resulted in the bounty of a similarly endowed California, realizes that it is not its land or people, but its *culture* that holds the country back. Out of envy or spite, there are many in Mexico who experience *schadenfreude* at the problems that arise when the continent's poorest and mostly illiterate head north to perplex the richest and most sophisticated. If America once invaded Mexico and hurt its pride, Mexico has now invaded America—but with millions rather than thousands, and as an occupying force that plans to stay. Anytime great wealth is juxtaposed to abject failure—the former Berlin, Hong Kong and communist China, the Koreas, Israel and the West Bank, southern Europe and northern Africa are good examples—sparks can fly. And Mexico is Catholic, America mostly Protestant or secular. The former believes fate is set at birth, the latter that man earns his condition mostly here on earth. All this and more contributes to making Mexico a special case. But there is a final consideration on America's part that has also made Mexico singular.

In the last twenty years we have seen a disingenuous new motto, "the borders crossed us, not we the borders," proclaimed by Mexicans both in California and in Mexico—or as Professor Truxillo of the University of New Mexico put it, "Southwest Chicanos and Norteño Mexicanos are becoming one people again." Note the key word *again*, and his care to say "Southwest *Chicanos*" rather than "Southwest Americans."

But we should remember that as recently as 1970 there were only 800,000 Mexican citizen immigrants in the United States. Remember that when the United States stole California there were fewer than 10,000 Mexicans living in a vast uninhabited area, one that itself had been stolen from Spain, which in turn had stolen it from the Indians. And recall that the parents or grandparents of 95 percent of California's current adult Mexicans were born in Mexico. The murky idea behind "the borders crossed us" is that the vast American Southwest was once part of a heavily populated Hispanic kingdom, nation or hegemony— use whatever term you will—and today, slowly, through the agency of peaceful and inevitable historical change is righteously reverting to its former and proper status. Look at a Chicano studies text and you see the map of the original Nuevo California that includes not just the present-day state, but all of Nevada, Arizona, Utah, parts of New Mexico, Colorado and even southern Wyoming!—as if there were once thousands of prosperous Mexicans plying their culture in a vast Hispanic American North.

A recent Zogby poll revealed that 58 percent of Mexican citizens believe that "the territory of the United States' Southwest rightfully belongs to Mexico." In contrast, the same poll showed that 68 percent of Americans want the U.S. military deployed on the border to keep illegal aliens out. Thucydides would conclude that with contrasting attitudes like that, you have the ingredients for a war of some sort—if not waged conventionally, then perhaps demographically.

Few in Mexico who entertain the zany irredentist vision of Nuevo California think such a process out carefully, and do not quite know what the eventual condition of the border zone between us will be—a greater Mexico, a simple assimilation of millions of brown gringos, or a new intermediary state of Mexifornia, with affinities to both countries and full allegiance to neither. It is common to hear those millions who come here slander Mexico to their new neighbors—which is logical, given their brutal treatment and low expectations back there; but just as frequently, nostalgia and romance gradually take over and make Mexico more attractive as it grows more distant. Thus to the Mexican government, the presence of millions of its nationals in the world's wealthiest country next door surely has more positive than negative consequences. Its expatriates naturally will at first lobby for concessions on everything from immigration to NAFTA, and ultimately, in theory, staff the government of California with Spanish-speaking officials sympathetic to close ties with Mexico City. Yet the lesson remains: Mexico is likable only from a safe distance.

Mexico's entire *image* has changed in our schools and popular culture. We went without a blink from racist pictures of a sleepy, mustachioed man in sombrero and poncho under a tree in the pueblo's plaza, to the other extreme of students dressed in Aztec costumes talking about Mexican law codes in the university free speech area. The former was cruel and insensitive, but at least it gave the immigrant a negative push to assimilate into the culture of his new land; the latter is comically ahistorical and ensures separatism and hence failure.

Instead of growing more distant, this newly romanticized Mexico of primal force and natural virtue has made strong claims on the heart of the new arrival, and thus has been ever more deleterious to his odyssey of becoming an American. Mexicans here can vote for candidates there. They see contenders for the presidency of Mexico campaigning in their American barrios. So even as they remain permanent residents of America, they continue to be civic participants of Mexico in absentia. Once they are free from their oppressive government, they reinvent Mexico as a nurturing landscape that obliterates the kleptocracy it actually is. The past corruption of politics and economics is forgotten in more hospitable surroundings, replaced by the romance of a distant culture. In a world where "all cultures are equal" and where racism, corruption and murder in the Third World are judged by a standard different from the West, too many Mexican authorities are not seen for what they often are: apparatchiks and gangsters, operating without the rule of law, who drive millions of their best and most intrepid citizens away. Mass kidnappings, endemic police-inspired murder, and rampant human-induced disasters at home seem to make far less impression on immigrants than the failure of California to provide driver's licenses to illegal aliens or to honor cards provided by the Mexican government as valid IDs.

In short, Mexico, the exporter of human cargo, presents an especially difficult and understated problem in the present immigration quagmire: They not only send us their surplus people; they export to us their own national confusion and conflicted self-image as well.

TWO
The Universe of the Illegal Alien

How DOES THE WORLD of illegal immigration look to the alien himself? Let us start by being candid. Nearly all the fruits and vegetables picked in the Southwest, supplying most of America with its fresh produce, are picked by Mexicans, most of them aliens, many of whom arrived in this country illegally, by stealth or by fraud. The nicest residential lawns in the Southwest are mowed by Mexicans, again mostly illegal aliens, but also green-card holders and naturalized citizens. In most restaurants in the southwestern United States the dishes are bussed and washed by Mexicans. In short, almost any physical labor that requires little skill or education but a great deal of physical strength and stamina and some courage, and that pays only a little over the minimum wage is now done by people born in Mexico—some with proper credentials, others without documentation and with dozens of false IDs.

Young men and women from Mexico now take on tasks that whites, Asians, African-Americans and second-generation Mexican-Americans apparently will not. This fact is denied repeatedly by almost all native-born Americans, who believe—even if they do not say so—that aliens are taking our good jobs. But rarely are unemployed whites, Asians, blacks, or second- or third-generation Mexican-Americans ever referred by the welfare department to pick in our nectarine orchard. Once a confused carload of poor whites showed up to pick grapes and left after a brief rendezvous with heat and dirt—baffled that anyone would be crazy enough to do such work. The last time I worked with white farm laborers—other than my brothers—in the vineyards was in the late 1950s and early 1960s, and they all had names like Delmas, Otis, Rhoda, Everette and Velma, the last vestiges of the Oklahoma migration of some three decades earlier. My wife's family all came to California from the Dust Bowl; none of her siblings or cousins has done any of the type of menial jobs that her grandparents and parents were routinely grateful to get.

The argument that alien unskilled labor is a new phenomenon in America is not entirely accurate. This country has always welcomed in cheap foreign workers when the economy was sound and menial labor short. It goes without saying that if we closed the borders, cut back state welfare subsidies and raised the minimum wage, then American citizens of the lower classes or at least our youth might become grass cutters, bed makers and grape pickers. But none of that is necessary when millions of industrious and impoverished workers are just hours away south of the border. Yet the moral quandary we face is clear when we acknowledge that denying residence to impoverished illegal aliens—a move that would end their hopes of freedom and economic betterment—would benefit enormously the Mexicans who are already here legally.

There are thousands of idle American teenagers at the mall every summer; others are lounging on the couch, while some are hard at work in computer camp. But so far I have not seen a single one employed in a vineyard or an orchard, whose owners instead use—and probably prefer—labor from Mexico to prevent their soft fruit, and so their livelihoods, from rotting. The U.S. Department of Labor reports that in July 2002, at a time of recession, less than half of America's teenagers were looking for summer employment—the lowest percentage since it began compiling statistics on youth job rates. In other words, millions of Americans are not working seasonal jobs that millions of Mexicans desperately want. There is something deeply ingrained now in the American character saying that Josh should not spend June and July in a chicken-packing plant. Nor must Nicole be sewing casual wear between spring and fall semesters as a temporary seamstress in a garment sweat shop.

In the late 1990s, after reading dozens of stories in our local paper about a severe shortage of grape pickers—and then witnessing firsthand that the raisin harvest was a week or two behind because too many farmers were seeking too few workers—I once drove to the three largest shopping centers in Fresno. The labor pool there was astounding! There were easily two or three thousand healthy men and women under twenty—shopping, loitering, idling, chatting on cell phones and flirting at 2 P.M. on a summer weekday. Some had cultivated physiques with bulging muscles and were well tanned, appearing to my mind more than ready for the rough outdoors of the vineyard.

There were enough Americans within a ten-mile vicinity who had the strength and health to pick all the grapes on seven or eight hundred acres of vineyard in a single day. But as Napoleon said of war, the will is to the matériel as three is to one. Not one of those young men and women works in the fields. Their parents may complain about how expensive their school clothes and electronic appurtenances are, but still unleash them to the malls, while the farmers gripe that nobody wants their wages to do hard, honest work, even as the Mexicans are happy to do what others will not, and thereby earn the money to buy what others purchase through parental subsidy.

Ban our yearly contingent of tough, lean Mexican immigrants completely from California tomorrow, and I think within a year or two the state would be almost paralyzed—much of its food decaying, its hotels dirty, its dishes unwashed, its lawns and shrubs weedy and unkempt. Remove the young Mexicans and our professional classes would learn rather quickly that fruit does not fall edible from trees, that the grass does indeed continue to grow, and that trenches do not open of their own accord like the Red Sea.

Dozens of agricultural magnates I know have never themselves—much less their children—picked any peaches from their thousands of trees, never sprayed organophosphates on their vast orchards, and never even mowed their own lawns. In the great debate now going on about immigration, it seems to me vital that critics of Mexican illegal aliens at least experiment—if only for forty-eight hours or so—with working at such helotage. They might serve as maids for a day at the Motel 6, or pick strawberries to understand the issues of stoop labor, its compensation, and why people who wish to work find in America work that Americans will not do. We must keep in mind that unlike the 1950s, when only the elite in our country had someone else tend their lawns and baby-sit their kids, now millions of the middle and upper-middle classes pay aliens for such services—a radical change in the American lifestyle made possible by the arrival of millions from Mexico in the last decades.

So at a personal level, whether the present massive immigration is good or bad sometimes depends on whether your lawn is being mowed cheaply, or you are mowing someone else's; whether you show up at the emergency room for thousands of dollars in free maternity care, or pay the highest state taxes in the country to provide care for someone who either cannot or will not acquire health insurance; whether you believe that we are all going to be fine because an illegal alien becomes valedictorian of his high-school class, or that none of us will have a future when almost four out of every ten Hispanic students—natives, resident aliens and illegal immigrants alike—are believed never to finish the twelfth grade.

As we contemplate this growing complexity, it is worth considering the world as it appears to the illegal alien—a cosmos that I know something about as one who has worked in orchards and vineyards side by side with farm workers for much of his life. One thing this alien knows in his heart: There is a simple reason why Americans do not do farm work, one that transcends even the absence of real money and any status. *It is physically hard to pick peaches all day.* The twelve-foot ladder is heavy and unstable, especially when you must clamber up among the top branches sixty or seventy times a day and then descend with fifty pounds of peaches strapped to your belly. Our knees, backs and shoulders are not designed for such work. Still, you tend to run rather than walk at work because at piece-rate labor, you can make $90 to $120 in a nine-hour shift—if the trees are of moderate size, the fruit to be stripped rather than color-picked, and the orchard relatively clean of noxious weeds. That you are one ladder-fall away from the poverty that ensues from a slipped disk or inches from a moving tractor tire and a snapped leg are dangers to be ignored if you are to work well and profitably. The dilemma of farm work was never that it was necessarily low-paid, but rather that it offered good wages on the condition that one was young, healthy and able to move on to something better before old age and infirmity set in.

It can easily reach 110 degrees in a peach orchard in the Central Valley of California. The effects of summer temperature are made worse by the tall grass, the lack of any breeze, and the humidity of the stifling grove. There are other occupational hazards—besides the minor irritants of peach fuzz, dehydration, a rare black widow spider, and foxtails and puncture vines in your socks and shoes. Sometimes the labor contractor can withhold your check without cause, or deduct 30 percent of it for Cokes, rides to work, and everything between.

The *trabajador* lives and works in a world of young men. They survive for the most part as small teams, under conditions of illegality, apart from their families, and are prone to settle disagreements with knives and worse. Cash—for drinks, a ride, lunch and laundry—is needed daily, even hourly. Most agricultural laborers carry their wages in fat wads in their front pocket. We should never forget that as a rule, illegal aliens come as single young males (*solos*)—and in the history of civilization it is single, transient young men who build bridges and roads, but also bring societies their crime and violence.

For a day or two each month, aliens carry perhaps as much as

$500 to $1,000 until they send half of it back to Mexico. An entire species of predatory criminals exists in California that simply cruises cheap apartment buildings, corner liquor stores and rural markets, always on the prowl for industrious Mexican laborers. Such marauders are playing a criminal lottery, hoping that the young Mixotec they jump or shoot on any particular evening might be carrying his entire month's pay—and not a revolver. A quick stickup can net over $1,000, will probably not be reported to the police, and usually does not draw an armed response. We hear on occasion of the demented white boy who goes into the desert to shoot his .22 at illegal aliens; but the real killers and predators are Mexican gangsters who steal, maim and rape with impunity their own more ambitious brethren from Mexico.

The Latino death rate—both citizens and aliens—from homicide is three times higher than for non-Hispanic whites. It is daily fare in our local papers to read of bodies dumped in peach orchards, the putrid remains of corpses fished out of irrigation canals, or the body parts and bones of the long-dead uncovered by the cultivator. These are the remains of hundreds of young men from central Mexico who simply disappeared—shot or stabbed and then dumped by thieves and murderers. When I read of another corpse being found nearby, I wonder, "Who was he? What are his mothers and sisters in Mexico right now thinking of him? What does his village back home or his tenement in Tijuana conclude of this strange *el Norte* where so many fortune hunters such as this young man end up badly?" If my grandfather (born in 1890) used to tell me of his own father's stories of shootouts in precivilized Selma, I think I now could match every such savage incident with a contemporary account of far worse bloodletting, as our town returns to its frontier heritage after a mere century of law and tranquility.

If the body is in somewhat presentable condition, the inevitable appeal for donations is aired on local television and radio to send him back to his pueblo in Mexico. Children wave rags outside of shopping malls and gas stations to lure cars in for a $5 wash, in usually vain efforts to collect $3,000 to ship what is left of a young Mexican male back home. At the local quick-mart the cigar box has $1 and $5 bills piled inside, with handwritten notes appealing for cash. I note that there is rarely more than $30 at any one time.

Besides the stabbings, the drunk-driving arrests and the risk of driving at high speed on the interstate without more than a few days of automobile experience, there is, of course, the plague of alcohol. Latinos die from cirrhosis of the liver at a rate higher than *any other ethnic group,* and twice the rate of whites. The rates of gonorrhea, herpes, chlamydia and venereal warts are epidemic in the immigrant population of young adult males—and rarely discussed. HIV infection is also generally recorded at twice the percentage found in the native white population. Our social health industry—which daily publishes a myriad of details about farm workers' mental health problems, the pathologies of a newly acquired diet of fatty processed food, and the lack of good dental care—ignores the fact that hundreds of thousands of young Mexicans suffer from an array of venereal diseases. I have seen workers plagued for days by painful urination from recurring venereal infection, resistant to one-time and often improperly administered prescriptions of antibiotics.

Others only haphazardly take medication for tuberculosis, a disease that is thirteen times more likely to be found in Hispanics than in whites. Not long ago, Hernando, who used to come by to borrow money, peddle illegal fireworks and look for scrap iron, said his "little" cough was now "three years old," and swore the medicine was worse than the disease—and thus to be avoided at all costs. I apologized for not wanting to talk closely with him and holding my breath as he went on and on. Nineteenth-century ailments that are rare among citizens of rural California—adult whooping cough, hepatitis, even tetanus—are not so rare among illegal immigrants, who enter without the health checks normally demanded of immigrants a century ago. Thousands of young men and women are leaving some of the most treacherous and disease-ridden terrain on the planet to go north. A man's immune system does not shed viruses when he crosses the border. It takes some time—and a lot of tax dollars—for a worker plagued with intestinal parasites, occasional malaria and drug-resistant TB to reach a level of Americanized health where his greatest worry will be acne and allergies.

Subsidiary industries of illegality also tempt the workers—mostly the fencing of stolen property (lawn mowers, scooters, bikes, hand tools and such) at rural swap meets. When cash, not credit card and checks, is the common currency, and there is no confirmation of citizenship, then one buys almost everything on the spot and without proof of sale. And when an illegal alien makes less than $30,000 a year, he is more likely to discount the moral implications of buying goods that are clearly stolen from others. Receipts are not needed or wanted; possession, not title, is the rule of ownership. When I lose a valuable piece of yard or farm equipment I often venture two miles down the road to the Selma Swap Meet on Sundays to see whether I can buy it back at ten cents on the dollar. Shovels, yard tools, electrical tools—anything not tied down or locked up—have all vanished from my farm. Their simulacra are on sale in an open-air mart a few miles away at a fraction of the replacement expense.

Two rural households just a mile away from mine routinely arrange cheap, second-hand bicycles, motor scooters and power tools on their lawns for cash sale—no proof of purchase, no receipts, no questions asked. Just today I shooed away Raul Ochoa, who went to high school with my son, when he showed up with an entire set of hydraulic chain saws, clippers and other accessories—brand new, obviously stolen. Careless as to how to use them, he offered them all to me for $20, about 2 percent of their real worth. But then Raul was just released from jail for his second felony grand theft conviction, and had plenty of things in a prior cache to move before risking a life behind bars to steal more and replenish his stocks. The other *vatos* in his car, I noticed, seemed to be eying my car, truck, lawn mower—and me as well.

In spring 2003, during the editing of the present book, all the mailboxes on our rural road were vandalized; our shed twenty yards from the house was broken into and ransacked a few hours after four Mexican youths stopped to inquire about "buying gas"; and twenty-four hours later our garage had all the spare furniture looted in the middle of the night. Roberto, who lives half a mile away, said he spotted three young Mexicans rifling through his mailbox, but could not catch them on his tractor as they sped away with all his just-paid bills. I reminded him that putting his mail in his own mailbox in rural Selma was like writing a blank check to a gang-banger.

Worse are the meth labs that seem to spring up throughout rural California—the nation's drug capital for do-it-yourself chemists. Workers in these operations can make thousands of dollars in a summer. Such potential profits explain why the drug is ubiquitous on our streets and why aliens who use and sell it are cramming our prisons. Unlike the heroin or cocaine trade, meth is particularly attractive to the rural immigrant. It is usually concocted among familiar trees and vines, in a rented barn or shed miles from town, where the immigration authorities and sheriffs rarely intrude. It is a natural outdoor activity ancillary to farm work, likewise conducted in solitude and with the same network of smugglers and contractors known from the illegal trek into the United States. On two occasions, tough-looking men have shown up in my yard inquiring about renting my barn as a future "dormitory" for workers—code for a drug-making lab. If a man is here illegally and living in a stealthy world to begin with, having come from a culture where drug dealing and manufacturing are endemic among the bureaucrats and the police, then the occasional straying from the vineyard to the lab need not be so radically defined in Manichean terms of good versus evil. One year of drug chemistry might earn an illegal alien $40,000 in cash, and give him the much-sought-after victorious return to Mexico in a way farm wages never can; or, contrarily, it can earn him twenty years in Folsom Prison, a body illustrated with tattoos, and lifelong membership in a Mexican prison gang.

Despite the dangers and drudgery, however, the wage for menial labor in America is far better than anything earned in Mexico. An unskilled laborer from the Sierra Madre is lucky to make $25 a week; in California he can easily earn nearly $10 an hour and often more. To the worker, the initial realization that there is such an El Dorado is dazzling, quite unbelievable. Young males under thirty years of age in their first tour of duty in America seem starved for work. They toil ten hours a day—amazed that they have more money in their wallets in a week than they once had in an entire year.

I sometimes think that only the vast contrast with Mexico keeps the illegal alien in America alive; only the memory of the former harshness of real hunger, dirt floors, untreated illnesses and outdoor privies in Mexico steels him for what he must face in America. I once asked two raisin-tray rollers how they felt after ten hours of labor on their knees in 110-degree weather—"Better than in Mexico," one said. I thought to myself, "Well, better than in hell too, I suppose." I paid them $100 each, but noticed that their car's starter was just about out, and figured they had rolled all day for the cost of getting home.

To talk with these young men is to hear of extravagant dreams —all culminating in a grand and permanent return to their village in central or southern Mexico: a ranchero, a new block house, two Chevy pickups, alligator boots, black felt hat, jewelry—all the Mexican signs of material success in America. Of course, the university activists who see themselves as illegals' advocates ridicule such notions of instant wealth as impossible to garner through unskilled labor. But they err in two ways: Much of the wages for yard work, cement, roofing and farming is paid on a cash basis, without the deductions for Social Security, Medicare, workman's compensation, state and federal taxes—the miasma of debits that easily can shrink an American's paycheck by a third to a half. Our young professors at California State University, Fresno, some with Ph.D.s from Berkeley and Stanford, will be lucky to take home $2,000 a month after deductions—appearing on the pay stub in some ten categories including state, federal, Social Security and Medicare taxes, health, dental and vision insurance fees, state retirement, parking and union dues. Some undocumented workers in construction can put in 200 hours of work per month, and at $10 cash per hour they match the English professor—without the tie, the decade's worth of degrees, the need to master the lingo of postmodernism, and the entire drain of life insurance, lawn care and braces for the kids.

Second, there is the much-remarked-upon gulf between the cost of living in California and the cost of surviving in rural Mexico. Everything from tortillas to changing a tire is a fraction of the price south of the border. If the *campesino* can go south with a van full of consumer goods unavailable cheaply in Mexico—stereos, cell phones, televisions, washers and dryers—the daily tab to eat, sleep and relax in his home pueblo is otherwise rather low. The dream of the young worker, then, is that he might earn money as a Mexican in America and then go home to live like an American in Mexico.

There is also a third mystical force in play that explains the alien's zeal to work so hard to acquire American dollars for a dream of retuning home. Mexico is a hierarchical society, where skin color, accent and ancestry determine one's social place, from the upper echelons of Mexico City to the governor's office in Yucatan. Not so in America, whose crass plutocracy has always valued money above breeding, diction, education, even hue and religion. In this connection, I think of Pepe Madrigal, who used to run crews of some six hundred men in Selma, drove a Mercedes, had two diamond rings, and lived in a beautiful home in nearby Sanger, not far from my farm. A millionaire here—before the IRS shut him down for failure to forward the FICA deductions of his workers—he claimed that he was a virtual billionaire in his Mexican hometown. There, in the eyes of his former *compadres*, he was apotheosized from a rural *campesino* into a *nuevo rico* who claimed he could buy the entire landscape of his birth, its petty aristocrats, snobs and bigwigs thrown in for good measure. ("Hell, I'll buy the church and the padre too if they will sell it," he once remarked to me.) For the rustic Mexican who occupies the bottom rung of a static society and has virtually no chance of upward mobility, America represents not just an escape from drudgery, but the phantasm of redemption—a way not so much of getting rich, but of *getting even.*

Yet most Mexicans in America *never* return home permanently, and the dream of Pepe Madrigal remains mostly a fantasy; Mexico, after all, is still a class-bound society where an Indian with ample capital can never quite make it. Oh, they may go back and forth yearly, but few choose to stay south. And here we collide again with the dilemma of illegal immigration. For all the brutality of America, the immigrant senses a weird sort of kindness here. Or at least he senses the presence of a select and liberal group of Americans in health care, law, education and government who feel it is their duty to help *him*, of all people—the lowly immigrant! And their efforts are not paltry. The well-intentioned Americans can deliver to the illegal immigrant housing, medicine and food at a level beyond almost anything found even among the well-off in Mexico City.

I often fly eastward via Phoenix with aliens from Fresno on their way to Guadalajara; the overhead compartments on the plane are stuffed with wrapped fishing rods, fax machines, and boxes of vitamins and medicine. But what follows from that? Is there an ophthalmologist in the town square back home to treat your glaucoma? Can you show up with a 103-degree temperature at the local clinic and be given an instantaneous shot for strep, with free sample bottles of new antibiotics accompanied by kind words of encouragement from a Stanford Medical School intern? And will your children come home with notices from the local school advising you about free study halls, college scholarships and mental health counseling—along with a printed lecture from an ambitious principal about his own proven commitment to "diversity" and "the richness of a multicultural perspective"? Is there a chance that being "Hispanic" in America bodes better for your children than remaining an "Indian" in Mexico? The finest universities of Mexico do not scout out Indians from Oaxaca to redress historic imbalances in their enrollment; America's Ivy League does.

No, the immigrant senses that—whether out of altruism, guilt or coercion—the crazy gringos in America treat him better than his beloved amigos in Mexico. So it is harder than one expects to cut this new umbilical cord he has grown in America. Tricky also it is to forsake the mall, the summer blockbuster movie fare, or the free and modern emergency room. Mexican television in America broadcasts not dry notices of immigration reform or Mexican consulate seminars, but splashy Jerry Springer–like talk shows, where Chicanas with dyed blond hair, breast implants and bare navels wiggle in the audience and chatter in hot tubs, unlike anything that used to be aired in the village plaza in Mexico. America, it turns out, gets into one's blood. A Mexican once told me, "I'm Siamese twins—my Mexican and American heads so glued together I can't turn in either direction."

But just because the illegal alien visits Mexico without staying permanently does not necessarily mean he is happy in America. Within three years—five at most—a series of stark realizations about the United States begin to crystallize in the mind of the alien. Most of those under twenty-five that I encounter are perpetually smiling. They bounce, not shuffle, on the sidewalk. They laugh out loud. Not so their elders forty and above. I see the Great Awareness etched on their faces. These guys grimace and wave their hands in anger, exhibiting more frustration than can be attributed to the ambiguity of middle age. A Mexican male who may be fifty often looks sixty and walks as if he is seventy.

He begins to see that he is the beleaguered root, while a myriad of others are the fleshy stalk, leaves and fruit of the immigrant experience. He goes to bed at 9 P.M. so as to rise at 4 A.M.—unlike the others who profit far more and off him. In his immediate circle there are the contractors who take him to work and bring him home. For that easy effort, they make not $10 an hour, but $100. (Californians deplore the dismal safety record of farm labor vans.

Hundreds with crude wooden benches, no seat belts, bald tires and intoxicated drivers, overloaded with fifteen workers, overturn each month—prompting the California Highway Patrol to bring in new rules, inspections and education programs. We lament all that, but must remember that these mobile coffins are not "vans" so much as taxis, which can bring the unlicensed and unregulated owner-driver of a dilapidated $600 vehicle a profit of over $1,000 a week.)

The agricultural leeches are only the alpha, not the omega that surrounds the unskilled laborer. Beyond them is a virtual army of parasites. The coyote who smuggled him in makes tens of thousands of dollars. The forger who gives him the false identification earns hundreds. The landlord who rents him—and two others—the use of a bed, not a room, garners as much or more. The woman who provides him sex, the local market that cashes his check for a cut, the used-car salesman who has him sign twenty-two pages of guarantees for a car with a cracked engine block—all these and more profit from the arms and back of the illegal alien.

Soon he butts up against the bizarre and pricey world of white America—the strange country that sends things in the mail and on time like parking tickets, hospital bills and collection notices, and on occasion can haul away your car even as you sleep should you not pay the final $300. I have had dozens of aliens bring me all sorts of byzantine papers, from welfare applications to I-9 forms; often they are bewildered and at times outraged that such mystic runes should apply to them and that I, with a Ph.D., cannot figure them out either. Better, they finally say after I have thrown up my hands, to ignore them—or *in extremis* hire a sharp Mexican *abogado* who knows the ropes.

Such lawyers, in fact, abound for taking care of things that finally can no longer be put off—everything from workman's compensation claims to personal injury suits. Remember, the alien legal industry is a multibillion-dollar enterprise that ultimately depends on the backs of those picking, pruning and cleaning. Mostly, lawyers are there to "help" you find papers, bring up your mother, avoid jury duty, buy a house, start the process of citizenship, evade deportation—all at $100 an hour, "special" for a fellow *paisano*. The *Fresno Bee* is full of their ads. On Spanish-speaking television they are every bit as obnoxious as English-speaking shysters. They are amusing to the white legal community—snobs and fools who have no idea that a good Spanish-speaking lawyer with a mail-order degree who specializes in immigration or civil law can make far more than a Boalt Hall graduate in Sacramento's top firm.

The alien realizes that even his nether world of undocumentation is still not so undocumented. Even if he sleeps in a southwest Fresno apartment building, paying $200 a month for ten hours' use of a bed; even if he catches a ride in a labor van for $10 round-trip; even if he buys beans and soda in bulk at Food-for-Less for $100 a month, there are still those who can steal his $3,000 roll of cash—legally and with impunity—and all in the noble service of keeping him in America, out of jail and away from notice. Rodrigo Pena, a brilliant crew boss, summed it up best for me something like this:

> There are only the two kinds who go to the bank—those to check on their money or those who go to get some. No in-betweens. $25,000 in cash a year isn't bad, but walk into a bank with that and try to get a loan, and they point you to the door. Mexicanos are the only people with cash stuffed in their pockets and still are worth no money.

Chewey Escobar, now thirty-eight, whom I met when he was looking for work at fifteen, at last has noticed that all the people in the American Southwest who do the least sought-after work are, like himself, Mexicans—whether washing windows, making beds at the hotel, hauling trash or picking lettuce. Why is this so? Chewey has a vague idea that the absence of education, degrees, contacts, perfect English and years (if not centuries) of family roots in America can mean that you blow leaves while some pink person in slippers and bathrobe sips coffee and watches you from a glass-enclosed solarium by the pool.

Someone like Chewey cannot help but think something like:

"I work, she does not. I sweat and lift and pick, and they sit and talk." Envy, it turns out, is a powerful new force in the life of the alien—especially when so often he is not mixing with America's middling classes, but hired as a gardener, nanny or unskilled laborer by our more affluent. That I tell him there are millions of poor whites who far outnumber impoverished Mexican-Americans makes no impression; it is the contrast—Mexican help, white helped—that he is obsessed with.

Since the age of Cortés, Mexico has been a distorted medieval economy in which a few thousand manorial families own the entire country. But even this great disequilibrium of wealth in a feudal Mexico is not so psychologically injurious to the peasant as is the ubiquity of the American upper-middle class. In Mexico, real money is far distant, never sprinkled about the countryside in the form of luxurious haciendas or sparkling condos. The far fewer Mexican wealthy act differently; they live in castles, so to speak, and remind you that they are the *patrones,* and not the sort of folk that *clientes* can chat with between spraying shots of malathion and Miracle-Gro on their petunias, as they do in egalitarian America.

You can snip the roses of an orthodontist who is worth a cool ten million and yet stands a few feet away from you, talking on his cell phone. His garage, which you wheelbarrow weeds by, is filled with a Mercedes, a Lexus and a BMW. You can skim his pool with Jacuzzi and treat it for algae while he sits by its side. In fact, you may be at his estate—painting, spraying weeds, changing diapers—more than he, who after all must somehow pay for it all. In America the wealthy—often rising from the middle and lower classes—are ostentatious, familiar, accessible, and so a generous and constant reminder that while you may be royalty compared with those of your station still in Mexico, you, the service worker, are still a peon in the American plutocracy.

The alien's water is, of course, as clean as a millionaire's. He drives on the same freeway. His windbreaker from Wal-Mart looks no different from the Wall Street tycoon's informal wear. All that and more makes America the most superficially equal nation in the history of civilization, where skill and luck, not just birth and breeding, gain money. America is what Rome once was to hustling Jews, Greeks and Numidians, whose millions of sesterces allowed them to buy the privilege of wearing an ancestral toga with a purple stripe and a signet ring of onyx—to the exasperation of old Italian knights.

But again, envy—what the Greeks called *phthonos*—is not logical. Rather, it is inborn in man. You can have ten times what you had in Mexico, but still be miserable that you have one-tenth what others in America do. In Mexico a flush toilet, clean water and a warm bath make you a rural aristocrat; in America, access to such amenities is expected and considered only the beginning of the good life, not the *summum bonum.* How soon one metamorphoses from being a guest grateful for the privilege of having plentiful, clean food to being churlish because his house lacks central air conditioning cannot be calculated exactly; but the divide between appreciation and resentment is not wide.

Many Americans who live in suburban houses, drive SUVs and go to a fern bar for predinner drinks have forgotten this age-old elemental drive to surpass your neighbor in the most visible ways. True, Americans engage in cold war over the quality of a rye-grass lawn or the size of a stained glass window on an oak front door, but they rarely feel in their gut the angst over working hard and sweating, trapped in menial labor in proximity to others who are not—and who are quite oblivious to one's plight.

So the alien must deal with a strange new schizophrenia that begins to consume him. Success in America is too often a relative rather than an absolute concept—and felt as such by the alien most of all. We are, after all, notorious for our constantly rising expectations and appetites. Many Americans no sooner have satisfied their material dreams than they begin to feel either bored or furious that someone else—someone "undeserving" or "lazy"—has more.

As the illegal immigrant begins to learn about this strange new country, he notices another truth every bit as bothersome as the gulf between the sweaty world of muscle-power and the air-conditioned world of paper-pushing. The immigrant life cycle turns inexorably: the wheel of fortune tears him up alive—unless he gets off before it begins to go south. The world of grapes, shingles and nails is a young fellow's universe. Between eighteen and forty the shoulders, back, knees and elbows can withstand the daily hefting, bending and pounding. Such bodies are paid that princely $10 an hour precisely for their energy and stamina. Cuts and abrasions heal in days, not weeks. Colds and flu do not linger. Time in itself is a swirl of emotion and sensuality, not a period for sober reflection that money should be bankrolled while cartilage is still supple and not yet arthritic.

I know this in my own bones. At twenty-six I could sulfur 120 acres of vines in a day, racing the tractor in sixth gear to cover ten acres an hour, oblivious to a sea of chemical and vineyard dust, careless as to the effects of pounding on the ears and the shaking seat on the kidneys. I liked the fact that I was not behind a desk. At dusk I could hop off the tractor and shower, then forget that I had ever spent twelve hours on the same seat, losing money for the effort. Not so at forty-eight—two hours on the Massey-Ferguson are misery. Grime in the nose triggers allergies; ears ring for days from the blast of the machine. The body can take two decades of such daily punishment, but not four. With increasing debts and obligations, I am now very bothered by the thought that I lose money sweating on the tractor, and make money only when cool and rested and sitting at a desk.

All these contradictions the immigrant also slowly senses as he looks at the weak picker in a crew of ten who at age fifty can scarcely scale the ladder. He doesn't like *hombres* with gray hair on a four-man gondola team. They are too slow and don't carry their weight in getting the cut grapes into the pan. They shuffle rather than trot down the rows. They represent his bleak future rather than his optimistic present. There is a reason why *el jefe,* the contractor, has a belly, ridiculous snake-skin boots, three golden teeth and a stiff cowboy hat that would blow off in a minute of real work: he is fifty-five, not twenty, a veteran of the fields, not an amateur, and often ailing and wizened rather than fresh and naïve.

But the aging of the unskilled worker is not merely degenerative in the physical sense. It encompasses what one described to me as "the whole thing"—which I take to mean wife, kids, dog and house. A man alone may be wealthy even at $10 an hour; he is an utter pauper at the same wage with a pregnant wife, two children in diapers, and a three-bedroom apartment with a clunky car in the stall and one in worse condition on blocks.

If you chain-saw firewood or clean bedpans at the rest home, as a single person you can still go to the movies, eat out now and then, and put a down payment on a nice car. That freedom is non-existent when there are six of you who depend on the wages of house-painting and brick-laying. The greatest hazard to the illegal immigrant is a large family—the truth that is never mentioned, much less discussed. Everything that he was born into—parents, priest, reigning mores—tells him to have five boys, better six or seven, to carry on the family name, ensure help in the fields, give more souls to God, provide visible proof of virility, and create a captive audience at the dinner table.

In contrast, everything America values—money, free time, individual growth, secular pleasure—advises the opposite. Quite often for the unskilled laborer, five children instead of two is the difference between death and life. I must mention here the even surer form of suicide: the presence of not one family, but two. A common-law woman and kids in Huron and a simultaneous wife with eight more in Jalisco prescribe a heart attack at forty. A tile setter I know tells me that he works every evening to pay for the wife and three dependents in Monterrey, Mexico—and every morning and afternoon for the wife and twins in Madera, California.

Just as his body slows down, the alien's obligations mount. Such a physical metamorphosis is as apparent to him as a darting tadpole's change into a tired old frog. Quite simply, the last thing America wants is a Spanish-speaking man fifty years old with dependents but no skills and a bad back. He has a tendency to stay home more than he works; he is bitter rather than upbeat; his romance with America is now more like a nightmare. He can become a baleful influence on his numerous kids, who hear of doubt and anger, not of retirement accounts and a vacation home in the mountains. If we wonder why the hardest-working alien in California sires sons who will not do the same kind of labor, who have tattoos, shaved heads and prison records rather than diplomas, we need look no further than the bitterness of the exhausted, poor and discontented father. His back and knees, after all, won him no victory at fifty, but in his mind they won a four-car garage for someone else.

When the alien can no longer stucco a house or plaster a pool, most contractors must turn him loose—falsely confident that all those years of expensive deductions and bothersome paperwork should at least pay for workman's compensation, state disability, Section 8 housing, food stamps, welfare, unemployment or some other government dole that will keep a tired Manuel or an ill Ramon alive. Most aliens in their fifties and sixties who are worn out, obese, diabetic, alcoholic or injured stay indoors, do indeed live on some sort of assistance, and venture out for a day or two each week to pick a few plums, lay four yards of concrete, or dig some trenches for cash between afternoon cartoons and Oprah. Drive into any central California town at 11 A.M. and you will see hundreds of adult males walking the sidewalks, sitting in cafes, milling around at the stores, or loitering in front of their apartments—all of them not working, all of them on some sort of donation, and most of them wounded veterans of some of the hardest jobs in America. Our government says that local Central Valley towns experience a 15 percent unemployment rate. The naked eye suggests instead that a quarter of the populace lacks a full-time job.

Meanwhile, America needs replacements for these undecorated veterans. Thus an entire new cohort comes north to renew this strange, unspoken cycle in the traffic of humankind. In almost every city in California, there is a familiar street, park or lumber yard parking lot where dozens of healthy Mexican men, fifteen to thirty years of age, congregate to hire themselves out for a day as laborers—hoping that a contractor will bid well for ten hours' use of their backs. Because we are an instinctual, rather than an explicitly expressive, society, we have no placards on the border —something like the entryway admonishment of Dante's *Inferno* —to warn the newcomer.

> Beware all you who would enter. Here are the rules: You are welcome to work hard between twenty and forty. But then please retire at fifty and return home. Stay young, healthy, single, sterile and lawful—and we want you; get old or injured, marry, procreate or break the law— and we don't.

The alien soon realizes that there is also an eerie disruption of his culture going on in the United States, or at least a complete reversal of what passes for normal in Mexico. America really is a revolutionary place. The shocking thing about the United States is not its burdensome traditions and stereotypes, but rather its sheer absence of shame and protocol—and of much continuity with anything past. To the alien that means muscles and manhood can mean far less than diction and looks. So far we have talked about the universe of the male laborer and the drudgery of the maid or nanny. But another strange phenomenon is also affecting the Mexican immigrant, one of radical gender reversal. Women in America seem to do better than men. They stay in school at twice the rate of boys. To establishment America, an attractive Latina with good English is much less threatening and more easily assimilated than a sunburned and calloused *hombre* who has not learned to say much more than "thank you."

A wife, sister or daughter is less likely to listen to men while residing in America, more likely to make more cash—and far more prone to become an American quickly. If our culture prefers looks, money and the office over muscle, handwork and the fields, then a young Mexican girl of twenty in tight slacks who speaks English well can outperform her twin brother who toils on his knees.

Quite simply, the lifeline to America for most immigrants is often found in their womenfolk who follow the men in a few years, and who inevitably soon feel no need to defer to a male who makes less and has more trouble with the language. I drive from rural Selma to Fresno each morning on a congested freeway, fighting traffic with thousands of young Hispanic girls in new Hondas, on their way from rural towns like Fowler, Parlier and Woodlake to jobs in health care, law, government and education in Fresno. More often than not their boyfriends and husbands are back at home, looking for work or laboring for cash five rather than nine hours a day.

A final note on the turbulent mental landscape of the immigrant: The university pundits who insist that aliens suffer from the plague of material impoverishment once again have it wrong. Immigration is more complex and frustrating a problem than mere poverty. I live in one of the poorest sections of the poorest counties in California, and people of all sorts are just not starving. Wal-Mart is packed. The local Blockbuster video store is teeming. Obesity, not emaciation, kills aliens. I can go into town and hear no English spoken at all, even as I see women with carts full of food, clothes and electronic goods. New Kias, Ford pickups and space-age baby strollers dot the shopping-center parking lot. The new China seems to be supplying us all with the cheapest consumer goods in history, as everything from tennis shoes to television sets costs a fraction in real dollars of what it did three decades ago.

There has never been a more affluent society in the history of civilization than is America of the early twenty-first century. I would wager that an illegal alien in America may have more buying power in his pocket than a subsidized university student in Athens or Oslo. Our own new American robber barons may live on islands, rig the stock market and represent greed incarnate, but something is definitely trickling down from their malfeasance. In Selma I see vast new housing developments for newly arrived Mexicans; they cram the fast food outlets and carry computers out from Office Max.

In global terms—compared with life in the Congo, Cambodia, Yemen or Bolivia—illegal aliens in California are not materially poor. They may not have HMOs, but they are treated at emergency rooms. Their houses may not yet be three-bedroom, two-bath, but their apartments have carpeting, air conditioners, heaters and appliances.

Aliens are also consummate and generous buyers, not overly cost-conscious, and far more affable in the store than affluent white or Korean shoppers. For years I peddled my fruit at farmers' markets in Carmel and Santa Cruz. As a crass generalization, the Asians and whites complained about the price, demanded samples and seemed always to eat at least one fig or plum without paying. Monterey Bay housewives wanted special discounts for their lavish dinner parties. They asked a litany of questions about sprays, fertilizers and farming techniques—all as a prerequisite for buying $2 worth of tomatoes.

But Mexican shoppers who spoke broken English? They came up silently, put twenty pounds of fruit and vegetables in a bag, joked about picking such produce themselves, and then slapped down a wad of bills (always cash, never checks of dubious trust)— never complaining about the quality of the produce, the price, or their own poverty. Had they been dressed in white pants, deck shoes and chic sunglasses—and the Carmelites in garish, glittery shirts and cheap polyester pants—you would have thought the aliens were the munificent gentry, the Monterey Hills crowd the boorish poor. For a man who works on his knees, food is simply fuel—not an aesthetic experience, not an occasion to present an impressive table for discriminating peers, and not part of a holistic health program that prays for longevity.

There is another type of impoverishment, which I can also attest to from my own life between 1980 and 1985. Then in my late twenties and early thirties I never made more than $10,000 a year as a full-time farmer, despite two children in diapers and a wife who labored to carry the laundry from a creaking farmhouse to a jerry-rigged washer in the shed. The immobility of such a rooted existence, without disposable income of any great quantity, created a poverty of dwindling expectations. All the material goods in the world cannot disguise the fact that you are chained to your environs. You can have an ample beer belly and still feel hungry if your four walls constitute a monotonous landscape. For the immigrant there is a trip to Mexico perhaps, or two days in Disneyland just maybe via a Greyhound bus, but the alien knows he can never really buy a Winnebago or fly off to pick up a cruise to the inland passage. To enjoy the good life of the California native, this man would have to make $50 an hour hammering shingles and have 1.5 children, not six.

The world that the alien sees on the magazine rack in Safeway—Martha Stewart's flagstone patios, the Greek islands of *Traveler* magazine, the glossy ads for summers in the Sierra cabin—all that might as well be a glimmering on Venus. The alien senses that there is a vague, though very nice universe somewhere nearby where wealthy white and Asian people go—and where he never will. And that inexperience with travel, new landscapes, exotic people—a blinkered existence of never straying more than a few miles from home that most of the six billion people on the planet grudgingly accept as their birthright—can be hard to stomach in America when so many come and go as they please. There really is more to life than bread and circuses.

Those who have not worked for low wages at exhausting jobs without respite or escape cannot be expected to understand the growing sense of despair that leads to helplessness and real bitterness among those so much better off than they once were in Mexico. But when you are tied to your trowel or your pruning shears, the world even in America can seem an unfair place. Again, all the mature acceptance of truth in the world—life is still far better than it was in Mexico, one is free to make money and go to school and incrementally better his lot here—does not mitigate the perception that others have so much freedom while you have so little and will die with so little.

When I drove a dirty diesel tractor with spray rig hours on end, I would wonder at the insurance agents, pesticide salesmen and agribusiness representatives in immaculate clothes who drove out to our vineyard in air-conditioned cars and had the freedom to chat on their company's time. How and why, I worried in my immaturity, when a man sweats and works so hard, does he make so little, when another who is clean, fresh and seemingly listless can make so much more? Lectures about complex economies, the delegation of authority, rare skills and education, control and use of capital, free will and responsibility—all that wisdom means little if you are on the hot tractor and someone else is in the cool Lexus.

We should remember that fact in all discussions of the illegal alien: whatever the mess we may feel we are in, most aliens from Mexico, despite their hard work, will never in their lifetimes enjoy the lifestyle that most of us Americans have. In this sense, the reasons that they are in the fields and the kitchens and we are not, and the fact that they are better off than they were before are in one sense irrelevant; for they will still pick and scrub while we do not, and for them that makes all the difference in the world.

In short, this illegal alien business is a hazardous odyssey in America, replete with modern-day Sirens and Cyclopes that can lure the immigrant onto the rocky coast or even eat him outright. A few deftly navigate their way home, but more, increasingly, founder on our shores.

THREE
The Mind of the Host

MOST AMERICANS AVOID unskilled routine labor. It is not that we are lazy. No one, in fact, works harder than we do. Europeans and Japanese labor far fewer hours each year. Even our office workers are exhausted: there is something especially stressful and unhealthful about sitting inside a carpeted office forty hours a week between artificially cooled and heated sheet-rock walls, dealing with numbers and names flittering across a computer screen.

Still, most of us are wise to the pitfalls of our own system. We realize that there is a "future" in the antiseptic high-tech office, while being the fourth man on a cement crew or making beds all day is a dead-end job—perhaps permissible as a way of initiating youth into the values of discipline and hard work, but after the age of twenty a growing guarantee of failure in America, in terms of both achieving fiscal security and keeping an aging body healthy. Getting cash wages off the books is not a sustainable proposition, even for our young with good joints. The compensation for menial labor brings entertainment and occasional gadgetry for the single young male, but seldom results in a house, two good cars, and adequate clothes and sustenance for a wife and kids.

Because everyone has hands and feet, however, we believe that menial or stoop labor can be done by anyone with the proper resignation and permanently lowered ambition. Increasingly we realize that our own children cannot or will not do such tasks as part of their growing up, so we basically cover our ears and eyes, and let others do what they must. Thus we ignored the sudden entry of millions of rural Mexican poor. But what at first was a relief became a troubling dilemma, and is now a near-disaster.

We all can become hypocritical and at times amoral, admiring illegal aliens as individuals—housekeepers, gardeners, kids' friends—but feeling less kindly when we see them in long lines at the Department of Motor Vehicles, or scan their pictures in newspaper ads for Crime Stoppers or reports from the police blotter.

I start with impressions gained from observing the roadside in front of my vineyard. There are five stretches of replanted vines. I habitually replant vines. As part of that task I also put in new stakes and patch wire. I also fish out cars of inebriated illegal aliens—five now in twenty years. I own a very small frontage on an underused rural avenue, so I cannot help but assume that the phenomenon of illegals leaving the road at high speed is surely widespread. There is an unwavering pattern in all five crashes on my land. A large Crown Victoria or Buick Le Sabre of decade-old vintage veers off the road at seventy miles per hour, ploughs through the vineyard and comes to a halt three or four rows in from the asphalt. The vine canes, stakes and wire serve as a cushion for the driver, who is *never* seriously injured. By the time I reach the scene, he has hobbled off through the vineyard—leaving beer cans, his crushed car, and $5,000 in ruined vines. The car was practically worthless, but now is totaled and less than worthless—and of course without license and registration.

The California Highway Patrol arrives two hours later to impound the wreck for the price of towing it away. If I am particularly upset, I make a follow-up call and learn from the official accident report that the crushed Impala had either nonexistent or fraudulent paperwork. So I shrug and spend a day clearing out the mess from the vineyard, picking up the glass, plastic car parts, broken stakes and decapitated vines. Then in winter I replant rootings and wait three years for them to bear—and write off the lost income and added expense. If I tell the officer who investigates the accident that I wish he had at least apprehended the criminal, he usually sighs off the record, "What would it matter? When we do catch them they have no license, no registration and no insurance—and it's a hassle to call the INS anyway." One time, and one time alone, the CHP officer arrested the miscreant in my devastated vineyard. Why? Before he plowed into my vines, he had sideswiped a county bridge down the road. Three feet of aluminum railing remained enmeshed in his grill—proof, as it were, that the State of California itself had been attacked by this illegal alien and therefore was finally within its rights to jail him and sell off his wrecked car.

I once got a chain and tried to drag the wreckage out with my tractor to impound it for scrap metal—until I was told by the authorities on the scene that this constituted "theft" and I must leave the demolished car in my vineyard until the county tow arrived to cart it away and store it in case the owner should later try to reclaim it. The law seems to say that the vehicle of the illegal alien who destroyed thousands of dollars' worth of vines is more sacrosanct than the property of the citizen.

About once a month I also systematically clear the roadside of trash—not just the usual beer bottles, tires and occasional fast food debris that accumulates as if by a law of nature, but entire plastic bags of foul wet garbage, soiled diapers and assorted household items: plastic toys, dishes, boxes and magazines. Sometimes the litter is tossed well into the orchard, where it pops tractor tires and clogs the cultivator. About once every six months, sofas, beds, televisions, washers and dryers, and entire bedroom sets and dirty mattresses appear on our property. If they are clustered in piles, they must be removed within hours. Otherwise the neglected flotsam suggests laxity, and laxity sends the message that the road by or through our farm has become a free dump.

Twice I have caught the dumpers, who despite curses agreed to pick up their offal. Twice I have found receipts in the trash for power or other bills, and so have had the sheriff track down the owners and order them to come back and clean up the mess. But mostly I just pick it up and forget about who did it. This pastoral drama is endless, despite the fact that city garbage pickup is cheap, and county dumps are not uncommon. There are even plenty of big Dumpsters in shopping centers. Yet for some reason—perhaps it is an atavism from the old country where trash is everywhere dumped outside city limits?—illegal aliens still go out to the country to dump their refuse, furniture, cars and pets on farmland.

We currently have three dogs and six cats—all strays that were found half-starved in the orchard and vineyard, most likely left there by aliens. (Where is PETA when one really needs it?) My wife saved one of our present cats after it was thrown out into the nectarine orchard; its siblings were quickly eaten by coyotes. After $200 of veterinarian care for shots, congestive heart failure and pneumonia, the poor creature is not only at home with the other adopted strays in our yard, but almost fat. Years earlier I nearly caught one woman who left a box of kittens—three dead, the other two hours away from it—by the mailbox. And speaking of this rural mailbox that I suppose has been standing by the side of our road for nearly a century, we no longer put our outgoing mail in it—having learned that the red flag is simply an invitation for someone to steal the envelopes before the postal carrier arrives. Sadly we are giving thought to ceasing rural postal service altogether, inasmuch as thieves often hit the mail as soon as it is delivered. They take parcels even without monetary value—I have had two entire book manuscripts disappear yards from our front door, including an edited draft of this book!

All the endangered fauna on our farm—red-tailed hawks, great horned owls, kit foxes—have at one time or another been shot, their carcasses left to rot as food for the coyotes, those ubiquitous survivors which intruders seem to regard almost as kin and so never shoot. On my nightly walks around our farm, I politely ask Mexican trespassers not to drink and leave their bottles on the alleyway, not to shoot their .22s at quail, turtles, owls and ducks, and not to leave their refuse in the orchards. It is sickening to see the remains of a barn owl or a Cooper's hawk rotting on the alley-way, machine-gunned for target practice. But increasingly, keeping illegal aliens and Mexican gang members off the property is a hopeless task; in the banter that follows my requests, some tres-passers seem piqued that anyone in California should dare to insist on the archaic notion of property rights. One especially smart teenager told me in broken English, "Hey, it's our land anyway—not yours."

My strangest find one morning was a whole trailer in front of our house—not a two-wheeler, but an enormous old cotton model of 1950s vintage with no license plate or identification. Maybe it had once served as a makeshift neighborhood dumpster; maybe five or six families had used it for their own solid waste dis-posal. In any case, three or four tons of trash—furniture, garbage, wood, tree limbs, clothes, Mexican newspapers and magazines—had been collecting in it for perhaps a year. The tires were nearly rotten; one was almost flat. How it was towed there in the middle of the night remains a mystery. The monstrosity was impossible to remove. Garbage was stacked in it ten feet high. Finally, after three weeks, the county came out with a dump trunk and skip-loader and piecemeal hauled the rotting carcass away.

I couldn't help but speculate about the mentality behind the trailer. Apparently, after it reached critical mass, some people finally realized that such a stinking, noxious mess was unpleasant in their own environs—and so they decided simply to tow it out to the premises of a gringo farmer who would probably take care of it.

Three hundred yards away from our home, at the road inter-section, there is a memorial to a fatal drunk-driving accident. A white cross, dry flowers and a small shrine—the Greeks call them *iconostases*—all commemorate the life of an alien who ran the stop sign and broadsided a truck. In fact, if one looks for such little shrines, they are as commonplace now in rural California as they are on the roads of Mexico, wherever there is a blind intersection of two rural roads. Thousands of aliens who rarely drove an automobile in Mexico are now the inheritors of America's cast-off behemoths—smoky SUVs with 200,000 miles, club-cab trucks with bad transmissions, old Rivieras that get ten miles to the gallon, or minivans with bald tires and no seat belts. Forget, as environmentalists have, about the matrix of problems with smog control, gas mileage, licensing, registration and insurance—all the protocols that cost an environmentally conscious Californian thousands of dollars each year—and simply consider that our least trained drivers are now behind the wheels of our most lethal automobiles.

Frequently right next to this impromptu immaculate holy place is a sofa, rotting and full of vermin. It would seem that if one alien can find the time and the means to erect a neat white cross at the side of a vineyard and from time to time refurbish the memorial with hand-lettered cards in Spanish, surely another can forgo dumping a sofa on the consecrated roadside. And if the keeper of the deceased's memory periodically brings candles and fresh flowers to grace the site of his lost one's death, why does he not at least remove the abandoned sofa that mars the sanctity of his memorial?

There are now calls to supply illegal aliens with California driver's licenses—a last-ditch response to the growing number of immigrants who do not always drive well and rarely do so under legal conditions, but are nevertheless on our freeways in enormous clunkers that sometimes engage in an ethnic version of demolition derby. The problem with such a statute is not its logic—ease and safety of transportation for workers is never to be casually discounted—but its effect on the mentality of legal California citizens. When California children turn sixteen, they go through a well-known ritual of presenting a birth certificate to the Department of Motor Vehicles to authenticate their age. If you doubt the regularity of this drama, go to any DMV office and listen to irate moms at the counter on their cell phones, calling home for someone to go through the kitchen drawers and bring down junior's long-lost birth certificate so that he might at least have a crack at getting his driving permit.

But if no such documentation is required of aliens, will we then allow *all* Californians to obtain licenses, the foundation of our security and identification, without proof of their birth and age? Or shall we insist on birth certificates only for legal California residents, and not for illegal aliens? Shall we make life easier for illegals who pose the greater danger on our roads, and more difficult for our own citizens who do not? One of the most fascinating aspects of the entire immigration fiasco is the unspoken logic of creating an alternate universe for the illegal alien, in which our long-honored rules and statutes do not apply—a separate code of frontier jurisprudence for millions who, ipso facto, have broken the old law by their unlawful entry into America.

We are entering a cynical time, when politicians deal with the flood of immigrants simply by envisioning them all as future voters and enacting bizarre legislation to win their gratitude. Or is the case more benign? Are we simply so flooded with aliens that any of the consistency or respect for past principle that is vital for the long-term health of the state is unfeasible in the short term?

The University of California and the California State University system are inexpensive for resident California taxpayers, but not for out-of-staters. We have always tried to gouge nonresident citizens to subsidize the ridiculously low tuition we charge our own residents. Yet recently, this age-old two-tier system of payment was determined to be "prejudicial" to resident illegal aliens, whose families purportedly "paid taxes" to our state coffers. Forget about issues of legal status and the questionable degree to which undocumented workers are compensated through legal payroll systems rather than cash. And for a moment ignore also the understandable long-term and constructive strategies of giving reduced tuition to encourage greater use of the universities by Hispanic residents.

Consider instead once more the precedent set. American citizens from Arizona and Nevada who enroll in California schools now pay more than double what illegal aliens from Mexico pay for tuition. We are rigorous in determining an Oregonian's resident status for the purpose of charging him more for tuition, but lax in confirming the illegality of Mexican aliens in our haste to provide them with discount rates not available to most U.S. citizens. One out-of-state student at California State University, Fresno, bitterly asked me, "If I renounce my American citizenship and reenter California illegally from Mexico, can I save $3,000 this year on fees?" I simply shrugged, unable to tell him that he was wrong.

Our local hospital emergency room serves almost exclusively Hispanics. Among them are all sorts of patients with questionable legal status who turn up at the oddest hours to receive excellent medical care for everything from a twisted knee to leukemia. Not long ago, I took my son in for emergency stitches for an athletic injury and saw a drama involving the aftermath of street warfare that taught me something. I learned that the Mexican gang member may shoot and stab with abandon, but in the agony of his last hours he demands without appreciation or knowledge the technology of the twentieth-century American emergency room to rebuild his liver and stitch up his shredded kidneys.

The wounded *vatos* I saw that night might not know a pancreas from a lung, but they were secure in the assumption that the doctor—a four-eyed wimp of the type they habitually stare down on the street—knew both nephrology and pneumonology. In a sobbing aria of need, one of these gang-bangers shrieked, "Mom, mommy, *madre, madre,* they stabbed me!" His mother was herself screaming in Spanish for nurses, doctors and support staff for *"mijo"* as they peeled off his bloody gang shirt and his soiled, feces-stained baggy trousers—on his way into the antiseptic emergency room. The doctor worked with one eye on his patient and another on two antagonistic groups of rival gang family members in the waiting room—worried that a renewal of hostilities would break out in his hospital before the night's wounded were stitched up and sent back out to battle.

Equally bizarre is the American policy of granting instant citizenship at our hospitals to infants of illegal aliens. We see pregnant women with no cash, no husband, no English and no papers who rush to the local hospital at the last minute to bring forth a United States citizen. The birth is a miraculous event indeed, for in theory the infant instantaneously can anchor a new American existence for a full array of parents and assorted relatives of illegal status. How surreal! If an American executive and his upscale pregnant wife deliver a son at a corporate retreat in Cabo San Lucas, they are headed for mountains of paperwork and expenses. The Mexican government, of course, does not consider Joshua Evans III a Mexican citizen by virtue of the fact that he entered the world under Mexican skies. But even the American government presence in Mexico is suspicious and niggardly with its gifts of citizenship to the offspring of its own temporary expatriates, often demanding that lawyers present all sorts of documentation at the local consulate to prove the bona fides of the young American who had the misfortune of being delivered outside U.S. borders.

Like most Californians, I am confused by second-generation gang members even when they aren't getting ready to rumble in the emergency room. This is a growing phenomenon resulting in part from the fact that, according to some studies, almost 40 percent of both Hispanic aliens and Hispanic citizens of immigrant background do not graduate from our state's high schools within the normal four years, while over 90 percent of Mexicans of all statuses have no B.A. degree. Hundreds of gang-bangers venture out into the rural counties to fornicate, shoot drugs, steal, rape and murder. I pick up their needles and condoms, brandy bottles and tampons nightly near our farm pond. Some have tried to break into my house. At least a dozen have brazenly carted away farm equipment, stolen fruit in front of my home, or simply beached their cars and walked away. I confront them monthly—scowls, threats, bad looks and all—and usually reason with foolish logic as in the following propositions: "How would you like it if I drove onto your front lawn and stripped your orange tree?" "Would you like me to drive my tractor to your front door and park it there?" "Can I go over to your house and take what I find lying around the yard?"

Sometimes the Chicano studies lore has filtered down to the gang member: I have had block-lettered gang graffiti painted on our irrigation standpipes demanding, "Help the helpless." Once I caught a thief red-handed with over a hundred pounds of pilfered Elberta peaches. This young proto-Marxist replied to orders to put the boxes down or face the sheriff this way: "Hey, *stupido*, how you gonna eat all that fruit now before it rots? So just give it to people who really need it."

These roving criminals offer a stark contrast to their hard-working fathers and mothers—and make us wonder what is wrong with Mexico or America, or both. How can some men and women who venture north with nothing and work twenty years to near decrepitude rear children who not only will not labor, but instead fight and maim? All sorts of cheap answers are proposed from the left and the right: racism, the brutality of American capitalism, the emptiness of our popular entertainment, the pathology of Mexican culture, or the laxity of our own welfare state. Yet in the meantime, the social costs of having so many who turn so criminal, remain uneducated, and need highly trained doctors and professionals to clean up their mess has become exasperating. Consider a random litany of recent experiences in my hometown:

- A young alien ran a red light, hit my truck and attempted to flee before I called the police on my cell phone. He had no identification, registration or insurance, and was clearly intoxicated.
- Not long after this I was in a bank where I watched an older gentleman sign his name with an "X." As I waited, three customers directly ahead of me argued with the teller over bounced checks, missed car payments and insufficient funds—two in Spanish, one in an Indian dialect that not even a Hispanic employee could quite decipher. Forty min-

utes later I went home without reaching the teller. No economist calculates the billions that are lost in time and efficiency in California daily when thousands of aliens must have translators and be instructed in the basics that millions of Californians take for granted. Instead, we all obliviously go about our business and hope the old system can transform a Native American from central Mexico into a suburbanite—without impinging on his indigenous culture and heritage, of course.

- A visit to the Department of Motor Vehicles is an hour-long disaster. English seems not to be spoken on either side of me; the line does not move; and the customers cannot understand the myriad forms to be filled out for their trailers, vans and cars.

- My daughter's car was hit in an intersection by a young Mexican who ran a stoplight, propelling her vehicle into a neighboring yard. The Mexican-American policeman took no report, issued no citation and let the driver off—after getting her phone number.

- In a car parked deep in our orchard, a man of about forty was slapping and cursing a younger woman. Was he armed? Was she in danger? I approached the car, asked him not to hit the woman and then to leave. He did—as *both* cursed me on the way out, the victim far more than her abuser.

Such are the whirling images that now surround someone living in California, at the epicenter of illegal immigration. The other day I went up to my office at California State University, then to the library, and at last to the department office. It was late summer and the campus was largely deserted after summer school had ended—except for hundreds of young grade-schoolers, the vast majority of them Mexican and Mexican-American. Race seems the unspoken prerequisite for participation. There are literally dozens of programs for such underprivileged, geared for kids from kindergarten through high school, all well-intended and inspirational: classes and workshops in self-esteem, remedial English,

Chicano pride, vocational training, SAT preparation, Mexican history, Mexican grievances. Lunch, tutors, teachers, the use of computers and classrooms are provided free of charge. The message that I glean from the literature describing their efforts is one involving the primacy of self-esteem, a certain obligation on the part of others to accommodate Chicanos, the need for racial solidarity, and a vague notion that the spoils of California, for a variety of sinister reasons, are not being divided fairly.

My classics students, with a good knowledge of two or three languages, European history and Western literature, and with impeccable English, often find tutorial and guidance work in these programs, which all seem to have titles that include buzz words like "Help," "Pride" or "Diversity." The irony, of course, is that our assimilated Mexican classics majors make both perfect tutors and imperfect role models for these state-mandated programs. Their commitment to education has given them the skills to impress these young kids and their teachers—and the confidence not to need any of the very counseling, tutoring and self-esteem that they provide to others. In fact, our own students' worry is how to duck the separate (or, in the euphemism of our administrators, "auxiliary") Hispanic graduation ceremony in spring. When they have received fellowships for graduate study, for some reason, ethnic counselors and professors whom they scarcely know turn up to prompt them to attend their self-segregated rites to give proof of Chicano success and pride—as if the Greek, Latin, French and German they have mastered could for a single day be the approved curriculum of the Chicano-Latino studies faculty. Recently one of our Mexican-American Latin and Greek students, who entered California illegally wrapped in a blanket, was accepted with full support to the Ph.D. program in European history at Princeton, with additional funding from the Mellon Foundation and a promised slot at Cambridge University in England for a year. Suddenly he was claimed by all the professors whose efforts at "instilling pride," rather than teaching the hard subjects, were antithetical to the very education and discipline that won him such attention.

Professors and activists harp on the notion of blanket racism in admissions, but all of our talented Hispanic students accept that they are being given opportunities and advantages unknown to middle- and lower-class whites—deference in fact traditionally reserved for the legacy-holders among the white Eastern elite.

Whatever we are doing wrong in our California schools, it is not, as popular myth suggests, a result of doing nothing. If anything, the problem is one of frenzied activity—almost always of the wrong kind. Our bankrupt state at great cost, *in loco parentis,* has taken up the task of turning thousands of children of illegal aliens and resident immigrants into familiar mall kids with Valley-girl accents, cell phones and Old Navy T-shirts, who rightly should not have to cut grass and pick grapes like their grandparents and parents. They are given every sort of counseling, pep talk, grievance boilerplate—everything but a real education that might allow them to compete with native Californians. How strange that we give minority children billions of dollars in extra aid and education that brings them almost no real scholarly preparation, but a lot of resentment among those taxpayers who subsidize it.

I have reached the point where I now believe that the military would do a better job than we in the university do with young people of all backgrounds. I note that Mexican-American—and all other—students who enter our classes after four years of military service are far better educated and disciplined than their peers of similar age. They are reluctant to waste a penny of their hard-earned education benefits, which is not true of others who have grants lavished on them because of their ethnic heritage and the modesty of their parents' income. Many good-thinking liberals worry about the exorbitant $400 billion that will soon be allotted for defense expenditures; but they fail to investigate how much of such funds are spent on salaries and training—manpower rather than just hardware. In contrast, few are concerned how much capital is provided to our universities, both by state and federal agencies, that not merely fails to ensure real education or even reasonable graduation rates, but in fact may do far more harm than good by creating a sense of victimhood and a reliance on government largess.

Not far away from my farm, in the Central Valley town of Parlier, there are entire tracts of three-bedroom, two-bath houses available with federal assistance to recent immigrants. A new health center is blocks away. None of this subsidy was provided by local municipal funds. Indeed, the city government—plagued by constant corruption, recall elections and tribalism—is little more than a ward of the federal government. (Policing was for years taken over by the county.) The town is 99 percent Mexican or Mexican-American, often broke, and dependent upon state and federal money for almost all of its services. And yet it has nice streets, homes, clinics and schools.

So America really *is* endeavoring to level the playing field in one era, rather than in the traditional three generations of past immigrant experience, as it feverishly tries to meet ever-rising expectations. Nineteenth-century Italian families may have taken sixty or more years to achieve economic equity with WASPs, but America has now unleashed its creativity and enormous powers of production to attempt to reduce that race for absolute parity to a decade or two. Anything less, we are told, and our society is failing, racist or pathological.

African-Americans, of course, resent the Mexican immigrants' development of such a sense of entitlement, and make a good case that the wages of their own youths' entry-level jobs are permanently depressed because of cheap alien labor. They also feel that the increasing desirability of bilingual skills for mid-level state government employment is simply another roadblock for their own advancement. Asians are bewildered by our state's labyrinth of contradictory laws and subsidies. The older Asian generation scoffs at the need for any special state aid when one can open a donut shop, stereo store, auto shop or accounting firm—even as their highly educated and often professionally employed children vaguely sense that a system of racial spoils, in fact, might prove advantageous to themselves.

The new ethnic argument for massive government help to

the less fortunate is perhaps most troubling to aging white Californians of Oklahoma extraction, the millions who drove into the state from the dire poverty of the Dust Bowl and got very little in housing, aid or education from the state or federal government. Those who work in the race industry allege that the relative success of these onetime Okies after a half-century comes exclusively from "being white." But I am not so sure. Most farmers resented their presence, especially their bothersome accents, culture and religion. I think the Okies' achievement in assimilation grew not out of our hospitality, but out of our brutality, which altered them and forced them to be more like Californians. In any case, now in their old age, they are mystified by a world in which only Spanish is spoken and government entities require no proof of citizenship.

The Dust Bowl migration to California is strangely almost never recalled in any discussion of Mexican aliens. Yet the culture of Oklahoma in the 1930s and 1940s was as antithetical to California as are Mexico's present customs. The arrivals then were, if anything, hungrier than today's migrants, and their own efforts at assimilation as checkered, as blocked by prejudice, cultural pride and nihilistic opposition. Today, Dust Bowl Oklahoma is a distant memory. Scarcely any Californian under thirty knows or cares whether his grandparents were kissing cousins of Steinbeck's Joads. I know my three children do not; my wife's mild efforts to evoke in them a smidgeon of pride in the Oklahoman heritage they got from her has been a total failure. But then it has been a halfhearted effort all along, since she was a product of an educational system that taught all of us to shed the past, to forget rather than nurse our wounds, and to embrace the future.

FOUR
The Old Simplicity That Worked

THE NEW MYTHOLOGY of La Raza taught in our colleges and universities goes something like this: California was and is an utterly racist state. Its myriad of laws and protocols stymied Mexican aspirations for a century and a half until the rise in the 1970s of militant interest groups—MEChA (*Movimiento Estudiantil Chicano de Aztlán*), MAPA (Mexican-American Political Association), the United Farm Workers and La Raza studies departments everywhere. They alone finally, and only through protest, agitation and occasional violence, have just started to change the complexion of California by insisting on more balanced and sensitive educational programs, coupled with a vast safety net of state assistance and federal affirmative action preferences to redress past injustices. All this was in rightful recompense for the theft of California from Mexico. Under this regime—intellectual and literal—today's massive illegal immigration is seen as just deserts in returning the American Southwest to its proper cultural foundations.

What has been the result of *la causa*? Has the lot of Hispanics—gauged by graduation rates from high school, percentages with college degrees, per capita crime statistics vis-à-vis whites and Asians—improved through these efforts to renew ethnic pride and force society to recognize past Chicano icons from Joaquín Murrieta to Caesar Chavez?

Unfortunately, *nearly the opposite is true.* Three decades after the rise of the new militancy and separatism, along with unchecked immigration, Hispanics have the highest dropout rates from high school and the lowest percentages of bachelor's degrees of any ethnic group in the state. For all the good intentions, outreach programs, city-sponsored Cinco de Mayos, Caesar Chavez state holidays and eponymous boulevards and billions of dollars in entitlements, the government—alas!—apparently does not have the power to create instantaneous parity by fiat. Indeed, in our collective efforts to be angelic we can sometimes be devilish by establishing the principle that the state is responsible for an individual's success or failure.

The key achievement of all these militant groups was the promulgation of a partial truth, which by its very incompleteness became part of today's Big Lie. Racism, discrimination, labor exploitation—these and more, of course, have been the burdens of the Mexican-American experience. They are also universal pathologies, and quite predictable given the peculiar relationship between a vast democratic and capitalist American nation and an autocratic, economically backward Mexico. But instead of being pondered in that light, these shortcomings are defined as uniquely the sins of white Americans.

The result of the whitewashed new history is that Aztec cannibalism and human sacrifice (especially at the dedication of the great pyramid of Huitzilopochtli in 1487) on a scale approaching the daily murder rate at Auschwitz are seldom discussed as a part of the Mexican past. While Cortés is loudly condemned, we do not hear that the Tlaxcaltecs and other tribes considered the Europeans saviors rather than enslavers. Terrorist organizations of the late nineteenth century like the Gorras Blancas and the Mano Negra are romanticized. The everyday killer Joaquín Murrieta becomes a modern-day Robin Hood who acted on behalf of *his people.* Endemic and historic Mexican discrimination—either on the basis of skin color (*zambos* or *negras*) or class (*surrumatos*)—is passed over. We are not often told of the racist, anti-Semitic and essentially fascist Sinarquismo movement of the early twentieth century, which favored both Prussian militarism and later German Nazism and claimed half a million supporters in Mexico and thousands north of the border. Reies López Tijerina has made a comeback, a popular folk icon in my college days, with his silly lawsuits about reclaiming "Chicano land" from present-day New Mexicans, including efforts to annex the Kit Carson National Forest to help create a vast racial state of "Aztlan." Yet rarely do the commentators who have resurrected Tijerina for their pantheon of brown heroes point out that his broadsides were racist to the core and laced with anti-Semitism. Few today discuss how the UFW failed because of its corruption and misappropriation of workers' funds—and its often bizarre antics such as forcing employees to undergo Synanon-inspired coercive training.

Mexican pathology is ignored in a monolithic caricature of the often heartbreaking history of the border, and so too are the early American efforts at redressing racism: the California Mexican Fact-Finding Committee, the state high court's reversal of the Sleepy Lagoon murder case, and the efforts of Anglos like Carey McWilliams and Alice Greenfield to champion Mexican causes. We know that easy therapy rather than complex tragedy brings dividends under the present system of racial antagonism in our universities, but does it bring college graduation rates above 7 or 8 percent as well? The terrible suspicion remains that by not emphasizing and promoting traditional education to young Latinos—broad classes in history, logic, philosophy, Western civilization, literature and classics—Chicano leaders ensure a constituency that simply does not possess the learning to question the one-dimensional history and cardboard-cutout heroes and villains that these leaders force-feed them.

Most past segregation was cultural rather than racial, and thus rarely absolute, since anyone who somehow got education, money and a nice house was accepted as mainstream. But even forty years ago there was certainly not much institutionalized racism left. My father's closest friend on the local junior college faculty, Ray Velasco, was a well-respected physics teacher in 1962. Even a small, conservative rural town like Selma was openly even-handed: In 1965 our top drama student in the fourth grade was Hilario Montoya. Our head football coach thirty-five years ago was Mexican-American. My high-school girlfriend, Ellen Martinez, received a full-ride scholarship to UC Santa Cruz in 1971. Our student body president in 1972 was Mexican-American.

At the acme of the La Raza movement of the 1960s and 1970s, so-called Hispanics had been in the mainstream of American life for years and had found their talent widely appreciated by all races—the best-selling recording artists Herb Alpert, Linda Ronstadt, Richie Valens, Freddie Fender and Joan Baez, the mega-stars Anthony Quinn and Ricardo Montalban, the actresses Raquel (Tejada) Welch, Chita Rivera and Rita Moreno, television icons like Freddie Prinze, Cheech Marin, the great Roberto Clemente, Orlando Cepeda, Tony Oliva and Jim Plunkett, tennis stars such as Rosie Casals, Pancho Gonzales, the famous coaches Tom Flores and Pancho Segura and the golfers Lee Trevino, Chi Chi Rodriguez and Nancy Lopez. And all this success came well before Selena, Fernando Valenzuela and Jennifer Lopez, and without the need of activists like Luis Valdez or Corky Gonzales. Most Americans did not know whether such heroes were Cuban, Puerto Rican or Mexican—and didn't much care, inasmuch as they were interested in talent, not race.

Hispanics were not always commensurately represented in all American institutions, but notable examples like those above could be multiplied ad infinitem, suggesting that roadblocks were not legal or institutional, but the inevitable social prejudices typical of dominant cultures the world over, which tend to react against their minorities (though elsewhere with autocratic government sanction that thwarts the possibility of amendment by a maturing and more tolerant citizenry). So when today's social critics talk of segregated swimming pools, race wars, and a scary atmosphere for Mexicans akin to the Deep South of segregation days, they are largely talking of a time long before Desi Arnaz and Jose Ferrer.

Until 1970, California dealt with rising Mexican immigration the way it handled the lesser influx of Asians, Sikhs, Armenians and all other mass arrivals of immigrants—with rather unapologetically coarse efforts to insist on assimilation. Behind such a one-dimensional policy there were simplistic but unmistakable assumptions about the immigrant: he was here to stay and become an American, not to go back and forth between the old and the new country. He was to become one of us, not we one of him. He was here because he chose to be here, and so was required to learn about us, not we about him.

An underlying supposition in that rather unsophisticated thinking was the prime theorem: *the United States is a place far superior to Mexico.* Otherwise the immigrant would have stayed put and we would instead have joined him, and thus we would have been his guests there, rather than his hosts here. A corollary was no less important in the mind of the Californian: if we changed so as to accommodate the Mexican alien, then logically he would have no need to come here, since he was voting with his feet to reject Mexican culture, not replicate it. As a Mexican friend admitted to me in a moment of candor, "If you let us make California into Mexico, we will just go to Oregon. If we turn Oregon into Mexico, we'll stampede our way into Washington. If we turn Washington into Mexico, we'll sneak into Canada." What he meant, I think, is that the preservation of American society in its present form—democracy, freedom, uncensored media, diversity in politics, religion and ethnicity, open markets, private property, a vibrant middle class, secular government, civic and judicial audit and more—was attractive to brave *Mexicanos* stuck in Mexico. They saw America as antithetical to their homeland, and thus their last and only hope.

What was all this chauvinistic and self-acclaimed sense of "superiority" of the United States over Mexico really about? Surely it was not based on racial or genetic pseudoscience, for even racist Californians conceded that many Mexican immigrants, against great odds, soon found parity in every sense with native

Californians. Rather the difference was empirically based and multifaceted—legal, economic, religious, historical, cultural and political. Our courts, it was once agreed, were less likely to be corrupt and tended to be systematic and public, not secretive, haphazard and capricious. Our police could be corrupt, but petty bribery was the exception, not the rule, and they did not assassinate reformers with regularity and impunity. There was nothing quite like the *mordida* in America—the "bite" put on citizens by every government official; those caught taking money were usually shamed and retired or jailed. Our police today are not escorting cocaine dealers and using squad cars to provide security for heroin smugglers on a regular basis.

Our religions were diverse—from eccentric Christian fundamentalists and persecuted Mormons to almost secular Unitarians and Congregationalists—not monolithic parishes. The many branches of Protestantism taught various and sometimes quite contrary doctrines concerning God's grace in this world and the next. Catholicism was more likely to suggest that the ills and inequities of this world would be redressed in the next; in the days before liberation theology, the grasping rich would get their due when they faced God, rather than be held accountable in the present. Under the monopoly of the conservative Catholic Church in Mexico, an entire culture was taught that sex was for procreation, and the more children, the more souls that could be saved. In contrast, the American Protestant tendency was to regard many offspring as requiring too much time and investment from parents, siblings and society at large—an idea that Catholics considered silly and selfish as well as blasphemous.

According to the educational theory that once held sway, America was the creation of Jefferson, Hamilton, Franklin and Adams; Mexico was the legacy of Hernan Cortés and Pedro Alvarado. Pilgrims were not the same as conquistadors, or so our teachers in their pride maintained. We broke away from liberal reforming British parliamentarians; Mexico much later and with more difficulty separated from a more authoritarian Spanish monarchy. North America was opened to mass immigration; Spain tried to keep all but the Spanish out of Latin America. We were a temperate climate; much of Mexico was nearly tropical. We kicked the English and French out early; Mexico had Spanish and French in their country even in the nineteenth century. American settlers from all over Europe swarmed into a largely uninhabited, but Mexican, Southwest; adventurous Mexican families and homesteaders in covered wagons did not then venture into a largely uninhabited Oregon, Montana and Wyoming. We fought Germans; Mexico intrigued with them. American society at its best was a society of three classes, not two; in Mexico it was mostly a war between *campesinos* and their patrons, as society from the very beginning of the Spanish conquest was to be defined as the private property of the elite *hidalgos* and *caballeros*.

Ours was not so much a patriarchal society, at least in comparison with Latin America or the Arab world. Women were more visible, often worked outside the home, and were active in protests; not so much in Mexico, at least in times of peace. In the United States, private property, deeds and title searches were de rigueur; the rule of property law was not so sacrosanct in Mexico. A man finding his newly built house on someone else's lot made headlines in America; in Mexico it raised not an eyebrow. Florida, a long peninsula with an inhospitable climate, was settled and its swamps drained as it became a successful multiracial state; Baja California, about the same size and shape and also blazing hot, until recently remained mostly a parched wasteland.

There was no siesta in America; more likely you ate your fatty foods while driving to and from work. Various strains of our heritage, some of them pernicious and neurotic—from the WASP ethic to German Mennonite and Scandinavian habits of constant work—made us pay more attention to our jobs and income than to our families and recreation. Americans, it seemed, lived to work; Mexicans worked to live. All that and more made America, rather than Mexico, an often cut-throat economic powerhouse, where the system protected capital and property, the government dispensed largess at the will of the people, and a person was judged on his performance at making money, not his class, parentage, race or religion.

If you wanted to retire, relax and be accorded status and privilege for being older, refined and male, then Mexico just might be a better place than America. But if you were Irish, Japanese, Korean, African-American, Indian, Muslim or Jehovah's Witness, and wished to work and get rich, then you'd do far better in America. Any who disagree can ask themselves: how many millions of these have flocked to Mexico, then or now?

The schools, without self-doubt, often rudely and with little apology, dealt head-on with the contradiction that plagues every immigrant to America. Lost in an entirely new world that initially either ignores, oppresses, or discriminates against him, he naturally tends to romanticize the distant culture that pushed him into exile in the first place. I do not know whether my early teachers were conscious of such human subtleties, or aware that an excess of deference can encourage disdain rather than gratitude, that newfound affluence can create envy, and that every majority culture—even one that has recently arrived from Mexico and established an ethnic enclave in a small rural California town—tends to ostracize a minority. Yet these were problems and paradoxes that our instructors sought to resolve one way or another. They seemed to know that the Mexican immigrant could and should retain a pride in his ethnic heritage—to be expressed in music, dance, art, literature, religion and cuisine *only*—while being mature enough to see that the core political, economic and social values of his abandoned country were to be properly and rapidly forgotten. In my hometown the idea was to turn Mexicans into Selmans. And yet, in accomplishing this delicate task, our grammar school teachers of the 1950s and 1960s, most with degrees from normal schools in Texas and Oklahoma, knew far better the fundamental differences between a flourishing multiracial society and a failed and fractious multicultural quagmire than do our present Ph.D.s from Stanford and Berkeley.

On "Old Country" day for "show and tell" we all brought in our family's native dress, food and books to class—hardly a diverse exercise when well over 90 percent of the students at Eric White Elementary School were from Mexico. The student presentations were one-dimensional and completely predictable, as were the teachers' evaluations; indeed, today such a response would earn immediate dismissal for the teacher and hours of therapeutic counseling for the aggrieved students.

The Mennonite Eric Scheidt once showed us his family's East Prussian Bible and even spoke a few words of German for us—as he was politely reminded how lucky his parents were to be here rather than being caught in Hitler's Germany. My twin brother and I brought Swedish rye crackers, a straw *dahla* horse and pictures of Vikings; but we were hurt when Mr. Payne remarked that Sweden was neutral in World War II. We replied that all second-generation Swedish Hansons in four families sent their only sons to World War II, in which all saw combat and not all survived—a desperate effort on the part of ten-year-olds to establish their patriotic *fides*. The onus was on us to prove our American credentials, and we found little empathy by claiming to be Swedes and absolutely no guilt to be tapped among our teachers for their being somewhat less ambiguously American.

All of us, but the vast Mexican majority in particular, rolled our eyes and were nauseated when Margaret Olsen went on and on about Denmark, claiming that Copenhagen was cleaner than Los Angeles and that Danes were the world's finest craftsmen. We put up with her silly handmade Danish dress, but deeply resented the idea that anything important in Denmark could be better than anything unimportant here. Why else, we wondered, would her parents have come here in the first place—and as late as 1940, no less? But of course, almost every other class presentation was Mexican-inspired—piñatas, lore about Pancho Villa, the glories of the Mexican saints—and thus just as brutally reinterpreted by our teachers as interesting artifacts of a foreign culture, but hardly the building blocks of a truly lawful and humane society such as our own.

Again, the paradoxical mentality of the immigrant was not politely ignored and certainly not assuaged, as it would be today, but rather directly assaulted. The unvoiced assumption—a formulation of classic know-nothingism—resonated with us: *If it is really so good over there, why don't you go back?* Was this an exercise in American exceptionalism? Absolutely. Did our teachers lay the foundations for later chauvinism that might manifest itself collectively in what is now derided as American "unilateralism" on the world stage? Perhaps. But did the relegation of cultural diversity to the realm of the private and familial rather than the public and official encourage divisiveness and tension? *Hardly at all.*

The goal of assimilation that was once the standard, if unspoken orthodoxy in our schools and government is now ridiculed as racist and untrue. The result is that the very idea of both Mexico and America is changing, as is the experience of the immigrant. Instead of growing more distant, a romanticized Mexico is kept closer to the heart of the new arrival—thus erecting a roadblock on his journey to becoming an American. Those who die as Mexicans in California have sought neither to become citizens of the United States nor to return to Mexico. As a local columnist for our paper recently described their nether world: *Pensaban que se iban a ir patras* ("They thought they would go back to their home"). Apparently he was sad that those who fled Mexico always nostalgically promised to go back, yet eventually died in the United States.

Sociologists, the media and university activists now envision balkanized enclaves in America, assuring us that retaining the umbilical cord of Mexican culture is not injurious. Instead, we are for the first time creating a unique culture that is neither Mexican nor American, but something amorphous and fluid—the dividend of the multicultural investment. Whether you break the law to reach California or immigrate legally, it makes little difference in determining how well you drive, whether you send your kids to college, or whether you draw on the public services of the state. The *bien pensant* punditry—which lives exclusively north of the border, most often in white suburbs that are not integrated—will rush to add that southern California and northern Mexico will soon create their own regional civilization, perhaps even their own language and culture. An offspring not wholly of either parent will arise, and this Califexico, Mexifornia or Republica del Norte is not a "bad" thing at all, but something which, if not exactly advantageous, at least is inevitable.

After all, these pundits note, two thousand *maquiladoras*—American corporations with Mexican workers—are expanding along the border, creating the veneer of American popular culture over the miasma of a Third World infrastructure. They do not dare say publicly, but they hope privately that this new hybrid civilization—at least its water, sewage, streets, police force, hotels, universities, cars and banks—will resemble San Diego more than Tijuana.

A former Mexican resident of Mendota—now a nearly all-Mexican community on the west side of California's Central Valley—remarked to me recently that he finally left his town "when the last white people left." His unspoken, apparently racist, message was echoed by a resident of Parlier, another nearby town that has also become essentially all Mexican. The latter boasted to me that he transferred all his children to nearby Kingsburg schools where "there are lots of white people." It would be easy to dismiss such crudity as the false consciousness of a victim of ingrained racism, or to suggest that such thinking is confined to a small minority of self-hating Mexicans. (Or perhaps the more sophisticated might attribute these startling confessions to affluence and white racism that created better material conditions in Kingsburg and ensured worse schools and social services in Parlier.)

Maybe, maybe not. As I see it, what both of these very bright, proud, capable men instead meant was that there were simply too many unassimilated Mexicans in Mendota and Parlier to ensure an American future for their children, a critical mass that had made both towns more resemble those left behind in Mexico than those in the United States, and therefore less safe, secure and desirable places to live. The Mendota resident amplified just that feeling by explaining to me that he liked living in a community with educated doctors, teachers, small business, and English as the standard language—because "things work better that way." Or as my friend from Parlier put it: "If I wanted to live in Mexico, I don't need to live in Parlier."

The immigration problem is much more than just a result of our demand and their supply. And the resulting muddle arises not because we are too crowded per se. Japan, after all, feeds, clothes and educates three times as many as we do without the natural wealth or open spaces of a California. If we were committed to metering immigration and demanding language immersion and complete assimilation of all new arrivals, California in time could handle a steady stream of legal Mexican immigrants.

The problem, rather, is the changing *attitude* toward immigration and assimilation—making too many of us increasingly separate and unequal, and thus apprehensive that a big state with plenty of room is already too crowded for what we have become. It has always been easier for people who emigrate to keep their own culture than to join the majority—if we have learned anything from our turn-of-the-century arrivals, it is that assimilation is difficult—but for the first time in our nation's history it is now also felt to be easier for their hosts to let them do so.

Rarely now do southwesterners express a confidence in our culture or a willingness to defend the larger values of Western civilization. The result is that our public schools are either apathetic about, or outright hostile to the Western paradigm—even as millions from the south are voting with their feet and their lives to enjoy what we so often smugly dismiss. Our elites do not understand just how rare consensual government is in the history of civilization. They wrongly think that we can instill confidence by praising the less successful cultures that aliens are escaping, rather than explaining the dynamism and morality of the civilization that our newcomers have pledged to join.

Few in government or the media have a clue that secular

rationalism, religious tolerance and the chauvinism of a middle class ensure that we enjoy a rare degree of liberality in our lives— only possible through a foundation of material prosperity built on the sanctity of private property and free markets. Even more rarely do they appreciate how such Western values are not predicated on race or ethnicity, but on simple acceptance of a core set of rights and responsibilities. Few Mexicans could ever be accepted as full citizens in China, Japan, Zimbabwe or Saudi Arabia—in other words, in many places of the non-Western world that define their citizenry by the criteria of race, tribe or religion. Despite the campus rhetoric of resentment and discrimination, it would be far harder for an Anglo immigrant to be accepted as a full citizen in a Michoacan village than it would be for a Mixotec to take root in Fresno.

Yet through multiculturalism, cultural relativism and a therapeutic curriculum our schools often promote the very values from which new immigrants are fleeing—tribalism, statism and group rather than individual interests. If taken to heart, such ideas lead our new arrivals to the postulates that cause abject failure in California: "My home buddies are my only friends"; "The school has failed to help me"; "Chicanos aren't treated right and need to stick together." In a larger sense, if we were to entertain the attitudes toward women that exist in Mexico; stress the need to favor relatives and friends rather than follow the blind protocols of civil service; or copy the Mexican constitution, court system, schools, universities, tax code, bureaucracy, energy industry or sewage system, then millions of Mexicans quite simply would stay put. There is a reason, after all, why those in a rather cold and inhospitable Canada, north of the Dakotas and Minnesota, do not cross into America by the millions, while others from a temperate, naturally beautiful, oil-rich, mineral-laden and fertile Mexico do.

The answer to our current dilemma has nothing to do with race. It has everything to do with the degree to which a society is openly Western, and can thereby create a culture that trumps its natural environment.

How, then, exactly did the old assimilationist model work? As I remember it, simply and effectively. In our grammar schools during the 1950s and 1960s, English was definitely the official language. As a result, at our local schools that were overwhelmingly first-generation Mexican, one could hear *not a word of Spanish* even on the playground. Groups of four and larger were not allowed to congregate at recess. Mr. Jackson, our Arkansas-bred principal, gave us lectures about "rat-packing" hapless individuals, and swore he would whip anyone who jumped someone unexpectedly and with greater numbers in an "unfair fight." Anytime he heard that four or five were going to "get" someone after school, he offered them boxing gloves and said they were welcome to go against him first. I remember that those caught fighting with "Mexican" kicking instead of the accepted "American" punching earned four, rather than two, spankings.

In class, a rather tough Americanism was rammed down our throats: biographies of Teddy Roosevelt, stories about Lou Gehrig, recitation from Longfellow, demonstrations of how to fold the flag, a repertoire of patriotic songs to master. "America the Beautiful" was memorized including its mostly forgotten second and third stanzas, along with a dozen other songs, from the almost impossible to sing "My Country 'Tis of Thee" to the corny "God Bless America." (I can still remember the Spanish-accented refrains of "Stand bêsid her.")

"Manners" and "Civics" were taught each week—weird lessons like not appearing "loud" in public or wearing glittery or showy clothes; the need for picking up random trash from the sidewalks; and especially the avoidance of the "hard look" or staring down strangers with the intent of "being unpleasant." Thinly veiled, but never expressed overtly, was the idea that much of our assimilationist rhetoric arose in direct antithesis to the perceived practices of our many immigrants from Mexico. The *pachuco*, now glorified in our universities as the original nationalist rebel who bravely battled the prejudices of white America, was our special boogeyman in 1963. We were told that this mutinous *chuko* combined the worst characteristics of Elvis Presley with dangerous habits of gangsters from Tijuana. Did he assimilate, hold down a job, and appreciate his newly adopted country? Or did he foment fights, avoid labor, and wear clothes intentionally designed to draw attention to himself?

We didn't learn—as my kids do today—that he was a second-generation "Zoot-suiter" with an illustrious fashion, cultural and social history of resistance to the racism and know-nothingism of the United States. We simply believed what we were told and judged by what we saw—and what we saw was empirical, namely that *chukos* started fights and were arrested for thefts while the rest of the Mexican kids who dressed as Americans pretty much kept out of trouble. So we ten- and eleven-year-olds all listened when our largely well-meaning and naïve white teachers warned us not to "go *chuk*"—which I think meant adopting beetle boots, Frisco pants, long and oiled-down hair with a ducktail in back, baggy shirts, armless wife-beater T-shirts, gaudy necklaces, and assorted chains, switchblades and brass knuckles. When my older brother wore Frisco jeans on the last day of school in junior high one year, the principal in a frenzy called home for my parents to pick him up at detention immediately. I asked my parents if he had, in fact, "gone *chuk*"—to their laughter and slight anger at the school's rigidity.

Our fourth-grade yard monitor, Mr. Kaufman, furious that our intramural Mexican captains were selecting their team members on the basis of familial relationships rather than proven talent, told me, my twin brother and the three other Anglo kids to form our own team—as an object lesson. Then he lectured us on how nepotism and tribalism were a small step from racial prejudice, and how team captains who discriminated against gifted athletes with no blood ties could find themselves the victims of much worse bias in the larger world—and for reasons far more malicious than merely being from a different clan. These teachers were at times insufferable in their condescension, haughty in their assumption that they were giving culture to the new arrivals and thereby lending their "know-how" for "making it in America"—but make it in America most of these immigrants did.

The best speller was Gracie Luna, who alone of our class knew the plural of "phenomenon." Armando Quintana was the most accomplished actor, always beating us out for dramatic parts that were mainly Anglo. My twin and I thought it unfair that the sixth-grade football coach did not demand birth certificates, since we sat the bench while those whom we suspected were really two or three years older played every game. One football whiz, Raul Carbajal, told us that he was sixteen. (How else was he shaving when the rest of us, at twelve years old, had only peach-fuzz?) When I saw him at a local baseball game last year, Raul, now nearly sixty and a veteran of thirty-five years as a skilled air-conditioning mechanic, told that he was actually eighteen at that time. As we watched our sons play ball, he said that our teachers, now long dead, who bought him new clothes and drove him home were "great men and women."

What we knew of Mexico was academic, and came out of geography and history classes, not "cultural studies"—its major exports, largest cities, history before and after Cortés, names of the Mexican presidents and dictators, and so on. Our classmates filled in the blanks about real life in Mexico with patchy memories and exaggerated stories of contaminated water and crooked cops down south. When Ralphie Salinas left at the semester break for a visit to Mexico, he asked me to pray for his safe return. When he got back safe and sound, he sold us illegal fireworks, pornographic comic books and strange candies, warning us in a whisper, "There are even scarier things down there than these."

Apparently, our rather unsophisticated teachers thought the purpose of learning was to master the English language and acquire the rudiments of math and American literature. As I can best fathom it some forty years later, their aim was to create a sweeping egalitarianism, a mass of students who would reach high school all with about the same chances of success or failure. And so we were given demerits for mispronouncing names, writing left-handed, and other felonies like chewing gum, handing in our papers without our names written on the upper-right-hand corner, and wearing Frisco or Payday baggy pants and pointy boots.

Latinos were asked by the district speech therapist, Mrs. Albright, to say "A Chevy with a stick-shift"—a drill to ensure that there was no sign of a Mexican accent, and that, like Armenians and Japanese, they could filter undetected into mainstream society and prosper in the judgmental world of commerce. "You are judged on how you speak, and a big vocabulary will do you no good if you maul your words," Mrs. Albright lectured us each Thursday morning. The sixtyish, blue-haired therapist added that "looks and diction" were as important for success as raw talent.

Mr. Gronski, our itinerant musician, who rotated to our rural school each Friday for a morning of "Music Appreciation," made us memorize polkas, waltzes, Australian ballads, Mexican folk songs and black spirituals without including a single editorial remark about oppression or exploitation. He was teaching us the music scale, the role of half- and quarter-notes the world over, and how different peoples sought to harmonize, use refrains, and embrace or eschew rhyme. I doubt that many of today's fifth-graders know what "harmony" and a "refrain" mean, or sing many songs from outside their own culture, and yet I imagine that they are certified to be "sensitive," "nonjudgmental" and "diverse," and that they do sing anthems to universalism.

Most of the kids I saw every day—like most of the adults that I now see daily around the farm—were from Mexico, and there was nothing held back about race. Skin color and national origin were quite out in the open in conversation. We few Anglos in our class of forty at the rural elementary school were labeled "white boys" or slurred as *gringos, güeros* or *gabachos.* In turn, we knew the majority as "Mexicans," *cholos, vatos* or *chuks,* and their parents more respectfully as "Mexican-Americans." In those days I assiduously sought the etymology of "gringo." My dad didn't know, though he was furious that other kids called me such a thing. My mother said it came from having green American money and left it at that. My friend Luis Cortez shrugged and assured us that we were "greener" than Mexicans, and that "gringo" wasn't as bad as "white trash" or "Okie"—and less a cut anyway than "beaner," "wetback" or *mojados*.

Chicano, Latino, Hispanic, La Raza and all the other cachet words were as yet unknown. We never knew what *malinchismo* was (purported betrayal of the Mexican people) or *Tio Tacos* or *pochos* (like Uncle Toms), much less La Raza Unida, MAPA or MEChA. I never heard the rubric "minority" until high school. "People of color" was two decades away; our biggest worry was avoiding the odious "colored people" and especially the N-word—which the Mexican kids were far more prone to use than the few whites against our half-dozen black schoolmates. Few of the professors today, whose smug moral universe is confined to the city limits of Berkeley, La Jolla, Palo Alto or Santa Barbara, would believe that in 1960 using the N-word twenty miles south of Fresno in a run-down schoolyard would send any Mexican kid to the office in a way "gringo" or "wetback" would not.

Most fights were not racial. We in the miniscule white minor-ity fought with and against Mexican-Americans. As I remember it, the great dividing line for most rumbles was whether you were born in Selma or Fresno. Fringe racists, of course, were around. Mr. Martinez, the fourth-grade teacher, told me in 1963, "Whitey is through in California. Some day, Victor, the whole town here will be Mexican, even the principal and the cops." He was, of course, prophetic, perhaps in ways he never imagined. As if to counter such chauvinism, Mrs. Wilson, a Texas native, com-plimented those in the art class who were "lighter than most from Mexico" and "could easily pass." I remember even at twelve think-ing that her racial categories were absurd. Why should her own liver-spotted, wrinkled and blotted white complexion be the vaunted standard of hue, when half the Mexican girls in the class had beautiful, smooth olive skin that any Parisian connoisseur of beauty could call flawless? Yet on the other hand, it was Mexican students, not white, who insisted on calling Hector Bacho "chocolate" because of his nearly black skin. And they, not we, were cruel to Jeronimo Chapas, the only Puerto Rican among four hundred fifth-graders with truly black features, calling him "black Mexican" daily and even "Chino," as if he were some sort of bizarre Asiatic.

There was nothing of the contemporary multicultural model—bilingual aides, written and spoken communication with parents in Spanish, textbooks highlighting the majesty of the Aztecs and the theft of northern Mexico, or federally funded counselors to warn about drugs, gangs and teen pregnancy, and propagandize students that "The borders crossed us, not we the borders." Excused absences for catechism classes at the Catholic Church emptied our classrooms, giving us five or six Anglo Protestants a much-welcomed three-hour recess. (We also suffered through fish sticks on Friday, the public school's other concession to the vast Catholic majority.) Our principal worried that between Catechism classes, speech therapy and music appreciation, the students were losing two or three hours a week of reading and writing.

Growing up in multiracial rural California in the early 1960s, we did not merely review the nuts and bolts of the Constitution, or learn patriotic songs and brief sketches of Washington, Jefferson and Lincoln. Our discussions and lectures about American exceptionalism were not the triumphalism of a particular white race or Christian religion, but rather emphasized our own deep appreciation for just how distinctive the culture of the United States had proved to be over some two centuries. William Saroyan's short stories were much in vogue in our English classes. Much of his landscape was familiar, and his references to places in his native Fresno and the surrounding towns were known by most of us. Our teachers seemed to take for granted that Saroyan was critical of American society, and did not mind at all that non-Armenians in his stories could be portrayed as hysterically hypocritical and silly in their insularity and insensitivity toward darker others. None of us quite knew what the big deal about Armenians was anyway—

since dozens of second- and third-generation Armenian-American kids were in our classes—only that they had apparently once, in ignorance, been treated unfairly as darker-skinned people.

Education was presented to everyone as the great escape from "the fields." The Japanese and Chinese had picked grapes and peaches at the turn of the century, before moving on to better lives. The Okies took their place before assimilating and leaving farm work. Armenians now owned the very farms they had once labored on. Education, unions, intermarriage, assimilation—all these forces and more made grape pickers into prosperous middle-class suburbanites. Mexicans, we trusted, were doing the same thing: those who were educated did not chop cotton; those who were not, did. And chopping cotton, while noble, paid little.

In fact, agricultural labor was presented as the great evil by our mostly Anglo teachers, many of whom themselves owned small vineyards! Cutting grapes was the specter by which they attempted to scare us into studying: "Okay, keep talking during class, Esperanza, and you will end up picking grapes the rest of your life." When farm-laboring parents at public schools week came into the classroom, the teachers politely but firmly reminded them that as fathers and mothers they had to monitor their children's homework so that the latter might have a better life than that found in the fields. "Make sure Juanito speaks English at home, so that he can sharpen his American accent," they would lecture these exhausted and sometimes bewildered farm workers.

Today we would call such pretentious do-gooding a wicked sort of "cultural genocide." Yet contemporary advocates of state-sanctioned bilingualism err when they claim that assimilationists wish to destroy knowledge of Spanish. The problem, instead, is not that our aliens know two languages, but that often they are not literate in even one.

What, then, did we actually learn in school that so quickly helped all of us assimilate—or rather, what made the other forty students in our homeroom class of 1961 become more like us six Anglos than we like them? Take our lessons on the Civil War: We all were told that thousands of Americans had died to end slavery, an evil institution that was as old as civilization itself. We admired the romance and pluck of the South, but concluded that its cause was inseparable from slavery and so morally wrong that it had to be ended—if need be, through bloodshed. Americans, it seemed, could be terrible to one another, but eventually there were more good than bad people, who could use a wonderful system to eradicate man's sins. The "North" or the "Union" was presented as the spiritual predecessor to our own efforts to get along and overcome race in the turmoil of the early 1960s. Our class often sang "Battle Hymn of the Republic"—with a heavily accented Mexican English.

We all got the message of racism, slavery and oppression clear enough while still learning something of Grant and Sherman and Jefferson Davis. I don't think we needed to be told that humans were imperfect—how else could the Constitution of the United States have tolerated slavery for nearly a hundred years? We had all seen the demons within our very selves out on the Darwinian playground and knew that their exorcism was the work of all good citizens. Even in rural California of the 1960s, "racial prejudice" was stigmatized as a great sin, something "unfair" that gave "advantages" to those who had not earned them. "You're prejudiced" was a charge whose sting was the assertion that one was dishonorable rather than merely bad.

Jimmy Hall was the class racist with a strong southwestern accent, rotten teeth and battle scars. He lived in a shack in a subsection of the barrio at the edge of the school, a rural shantytown ("Sunnyside") where Okies and blacks had settled in the 1940s and not yet fully abandoned by 1963. If there was hostility shown to students by our tough faculty composed of World War II veterans, it was usually directed against him. "Be nice to Jimmy—his family is ignorant and doesn't know any better," we were told in condescending tones. "They are white trash who never made it," our Texas- and Oklahoma-raised teachers said about Jimmy. "I've seen his kind back home, so be careful, you guys," our principal warned.

The underlying assumption in making such comments to our majority of Mexican students was that *they* had a real culture and family stability that could lead to success, while white-trash, dysfunctional families like the Halls—a "needle and syringe," the rumors went, had landed Jimmy's sometime father in the "state pen"—were beyond redemption. The prejudice toward Okies is now romanticized and airbrushed, but I remember it as visceral and unending until the 1960s. My wife, who has this drama in her family background, claims that it persisted well into the 1980s.

Did our education neglect the labor unions and the struggle of the oppressed? Not at all. As the nascent United Farm Workers movement was capturing national attention by staging strikes daily right outside town, our seventh-grade history teacher was sketching out the dreadful struggle of the coal miners and steel workers, and reminding us how in a free and capitalist society the poor always had to organize to find redress from the powerful. Other mentors explained the unhappy saga of the immigrants—Irish, Jews, Italians, Chinese, Mexicans—not to teach the cheap lesson that America was racist and oppressive, but in the belief that our country was better than others because our parents and grandparents had taken it upon themselves to improve an unjust situation.

Caesar Chavez was, of course, hated by the local farming establishment—unreasonably so, for his initial cause was just and long overdue. At ten, I saw him walk with his followers along the old Highway 99 with a bullhorn and banners. At seventeen my brother and I once, out of curiosity, drove out to one of his rallies, got lost, ended up at a disputed orchard, and were roughed up by Tulare County sheriffs who appeared out of nowhere, drawling, "What are you white boys doing on this side of the picket line?" The less vehement slurs from small indigent farmers were mostly that Chavez was "lazy" and "never worked," rather than the corporations' wild charges that he was a "communist" or a "Marxist." Tad Abe, who had helped form the Nisei Farmers' League—a group of Japanese small grape growers and family tree-fruit farmers who wished to stop UFW vandalism—said that if he was once forced to live in an Arizona internment camp at fifteen, then by god the union agitators should be put there too.

Still, in the public schools we got a vague message that this hated Caesar Chavez was "standing up for his people." What that precisely meant, we were never told other than that it was a very American thing to "stand up for your people." I distinctly remember putting a "Huelga" and a "Boycott Grapes" sticker on the bumper of my cattleman great-uncle's car, which he unknowingly drove around with for two days, to the perplexed looks of his reactionary friends. But the fact was that the handful of us Anglo kids who lived on small farms with our grandparents, parents and cousins usually were not that much better off than the Mexican families who had migrated from farm work to business, the post office or the schools. I remember that when my friend Armando Aguallo visited our tiny one-bedroom farmhouse in 1962, he gasped, "We have a nicer home than you and we're Mexican!" And so he did, given my father's failures as a cotton farmer before going to town for work. In any case, we had no vested interest in defending corporate agribusiness and more or less hoped the "big guys" would be unionized and leave the rest of us alone to work beside people we grew up with.

Could it be that two of the greatest villains in the destruction of the old assimilationist model that integrated my boyhood Mexican friends into an American outlook and expectation have been big government and big corporations, both entities that have no interest in local institutions? The former finds power in mindless consensus, the latter in money, and both look askance at anything that poses an obstacle.

Only later, in high school, did I slowly learn why Caesar Chavez himself vastly preferred dealing with agribusiness corporations rather than small farmers—with giant, wealthy entities, not sticky little enclaves of cranky and always broke Japanese, Armenians, Swedes, Mexicans and Punjabis who lived next to and not much differently from their workers. Indeed, if he was ever to realize his ambitions of becoming the Mexican George Meany in charge of a vast empire of stoop laborers, then Chavez needed the opposition of an easily caricatured rapacious, racist, wealthy, white enemy. He wanted a countryside not full of small family farmers, but of a few big agribusinessmen. The agribusiness corporation was an easy foil, which under an avalanche of liberal commentary, boycotts and high-profile visits to Fresno and Delano by the Kennedys and other celebrities could capitulate on television with a wave of the pen, sending his own union millions of dollars in paycheck deductions that, of course, would be looted, lost or mishandled by an extended clique of his family and cronies. And so precisely all that came to pass for poor Caesar Chavez in the 1970s.

Meanwhile, our schools quietly pressed on in presenting their version of American history, including the saga of the struggle for workers' rights. World War II? We all reviewed the "Four Freedoms" to stress how we had no other choice but to destroy the Nazis and Japanese militarists before we could remake their countries on principles similar to our own—which, being far more humane, would ensure that they did not revert to Auschwitz and the Rape of Nanking. In the early 1960s we knew intimately the story of Hiroshima and the Japanese internment; yet we learned that such tragedies were not the sole themes of World War II, but part of a saga that included the sacrifices at Pearl Harbor, Guadalcanal, Iwo Jima and Okinawa—names mostly unknown to present-day schoolchildren.

Immigrants shared in these discussions. Almost every Mexican kid had a father, uncle or cousin who had fought on the frontlines of World War II or Korea. Our teachers were often veterans and appreciated the opportunity to tell war stories. One student's father volunteered to come into class and show us the manual of arms with an old unloaded carbine. Arthur Luna brought in his dad's medal during war show-and-tell. Mrs. Burton—I remember it as if it were yesterday—announced to us all, "Remember, all you children, that your parents from Mexico fought for this country so that you could have what they did not."

Again, lofty and simplistic? Perhaps. But valuable for eight-year-olds of all races to hear? Entirely.

Even on occasions in the higher grades when the majority of my class found adolescent affinity with past victims of American intolerance, most still believed that they were beneficiaries of a system that could and would evolve and thus always offer them more advantages than any alternative. A sense of humility and balance achieved through comparison with contemporary societies elsewhere, and confidence in our values, measured against a recognition of innate human weakness, framed all such debates about the American experience.

We once discussed a recent episode of the television show *Maverick* about an Indian woman named "Sue" (code name for Sioux) who, disguised as a white woman, as I remember it, had murdered a card shark for his boast of murdering Indians. The show's hero, Bart Maverick—remember this was in 1962 or 1963—lectured the congregation of miners contemplating her punishment that she should go free and that they all were improperly on Indian land and were more likely than she the real thieves and murderers. Our Mrs. Goddard, who led the classroom discussion, seemed especially pleased that we should know of the sins of miners and settlers against Indians, without suggesting that these sins exemplified the entire American experience. We forget that several of the classic Westerns of that age—Katy Jurado complaining of prejudice in *High Noon*, the beleaguered Mexican villagers of *The Magnificent Seven*, the sympathetic homesteaders of *Shane*, or the odious and racist cattle baron in *The Professionals*—portrayed Mexicans, blacks and the poor as noble souls or as victims of unjust white racism.

Given the current pessimism and national obsession with racism, sexism and oppression, it is easy now to ridicule as naïve the former trust in American institutions and to suggest that such recollections as those above are simply the biased nostalgia of someone from the "dominant" culture. Yet the positive impact upon immigrants of the traditional education that sought to make one from many was indisputable. Almost all of those from my second-grade class are today teachers, principals, business men and women, and government employees. If the purpose of such an education system as the one that formed us was to turn out true Americans of every hue, and to instill in them a love of their country and a sense of personal possibility, then the evidence forty years later would say that it was an unquestionable success.

In the tiny town of Selma, where we lived in the late 1950s and early 1960s, at the cutting edge of what would become a tidal wave of Mexican immigration, we not only knew that our country was different from others, but also understood why and how it was clearly superior. And the confidence that sprang from such knowledge, tested by criticism and supported with facts, gave us the ability to counter the cheap anti-Americanism abroad, and here at home to create a real sense of national harmony. Like most other Americans we saw the McCarthy era, Jim Crow and the sexual chauvinism that affected the country in the early 1960s as symptoms of the imperfection of the human condition, but curable with work and patience. We were not tempted to believe that there were better answers in other systems elsewhere. None looked to Cuba for tolerance of dissent, to China for racial equity, or to the Third World generally for gender parity.

The only thing that made us Americans any different from other people, we were taught, was our singular Constitution and democratic creed, which provided a framework for moral evolution. The promulgation of such a pragmatic ideology relieved us from the ethical posturing that would overtake the campuses, or any bloody effort to ram equality and fraternity down the throats of our countrymen with the barrel of a gun. So we looked back at the bad moments in American history for signs of amelioration, not for evidence that we must become revolutionaries. And we did not inflate our own moral pretensions by deprecating our ancestors on the frontier who lacked our material bounty and technological safety net, but often possessed physical courage and strength that we did not.

I know from my children that today's students see a different picture. They focus on dismal failure in the American experience where we once saw progress. We appreciated the slow struggle of politics and culture to trump universal human pathology. Now they are taught that bourgeois liberalism creates a particular American malevolence not found in other cultures and nations.

The victories of World War II, the reconstruction of Europe, the containment of homicidal communism, and the painful effort to ensure racial and sexual equality of opportunity here at home would have been impossible without an America sure of what it was and aware of what it had to do. Yet the self-confidence that taught values to the immigrant has nearly vanished from our schools. The results in the decline of civic education are unmistakable. It is not just that millions of Americans do not understand fully the mechanics of their own government or the seminal events of their history—57 percent of American high-school students, we were recently told, are now deemed "not proficient" in basic history—but that they also have little idea of what it is to be an American. Ask a high-school student to define an "American" and you will be met either by silence or by annoying catchphrases such as "diverse" or "multicultural," if not hollow references to being "nonjudgmental" and allowing others to "do their own thing." How can a society that is increasingly ignorant of its own past offer instruction to immigrants about the nature of the culture they must embrace?

It cannot. Consequently, we are left with one of the last great absurdities among the bankrupt ideologies and worldviews of the twentieth century: the present-day efforts of well-heeled elites and comfortable middle-class white teachers and bureaucrats to provide to immigrants desperate to become part of the United States every reason why they should hold themselves separate and not commit themselves to the new world they have discovered. It will be left to cultural historians in saner times to ascertain whether this self-loathing deprecation so endemic in the West today was the product of guilt over material abundance or of a genuine desire to reshape American society radically and by undemocratic means. In either case, the results of such bottled piety upon the immigrant have been disastrous.

FIVE
The New Gods That Failed

 WHAT ACCOUNTS FOR THE erosion of the civic education so necessary to sustain a unified nation that has no common race or religion? The first reason for a rejection of assimilation in our schools was ideological. We have not yet experienced all the consequences of the big bang of multiculturalism, authoritarian utopianism and cultural relativism—the isms that tell young people that facts, dates, people and hard data are either irrelevant or biased, or simply not facts at all, and that to question such a dogma could be "racist." I have had too many young students who mouthed clichés like, "We don't need to study the West," but when asked what "the West" was, were speechless and could not provide even a *wrong* answer. We have experienced enough of the assorted isms to know that all such ideology is antithetical to the notion of civic education, which historically has been national, realistic and in some way tragic rather than therapeutic. The old idea was that we were humans, not gods, and so we did not regard history as an exercise in deconstructing the past by retroactively apportioning blame and praise according to present standards of morality.

In the fourth grade we were asked to memorize the names of all the California missions. Protestant and Catholic alike learned that Father Serra was a civilizing, if flawed figure who tried to introduce agriculture, transportation and some refinement to a barren California landscape. In contrast, later generations have been told that the friar was a martinet who whipped Indians and forced them to convert to Catholicism. Surely the truth lies somewhere between the romanticism of my own education and the cynicism of the current indoctrination. But what is missing in the new dispensation is any sense that the world in which we now live—the cosmos of universities, the rule of law, antibiotics, surgery and eyeglasses—for good or ill evolved from the world of Father Serra, not from the indigenous peoples of California whom he may or may not have oppressed.

After the end of institutionalized discrimination in the last half of the twentieth century, our schools also wrongly took on the remaining—and doomed—task of replacing a level playing field of opportunity with an absolute equality of results. In a drive for near-instantaneous and perfect egalitarianism, there was a multifront effort to legislate and profess equality rather than simply provide the environment that would facilitate its emergence. How impatient we have become in our quest for utopia! Because of the rapid improvement in our material lives through technological advances, the fiction developed that the nature of man could be similarly improved at the same dizzying pace. It is as if emphasizing the grandeur of Aztec culture might make the shock of an Indian's arrival in the United States from Mexico less traumatic—even though all the protocols of the American public schools, from secularism and free speech to tolerance and rationalism, had no pedigree in Tenochtitlán!

The snippets of Old Country history fed to the immigrant like exotic hors d'oeuvres in his new world as a way of making him feel proud of his past must always be very selective, because the truth is often simply not palatable. Romanticizing the Aztecs, who were not averse to ripping out the hearts of virgins and children, and who were loathed by all the surrounding peoples they enslaved, is merely the most hair-raising example. Few Californians today realize that Native Americans were treated as badly by the Mexican government as by the gringos, or usually far worse. The

Mexican states of Chihuahua and Sonora both offered govern-ment bounties for the scalps of Apache men, women and children. The Chinese, who usually came to Mexico only as a means of cir-cumventing American immigration restrictions—hardly as oppressive as Mexican statutes—routinely experienced theft, rape and murder at the hand of Mexicans, all of which went unnoticed or were abetted by the government. (Even now, illegal aliens from Guatemala and elsewhere in Central America find the conduct of Mexican border guards far more brutal than anything experienced by Mexicans coming into America.) No California students today are taught that the Pershing expedition of 1916 against Pancho Villa—the purported *locus classicus* of Yankee imperialism—actu-ally brought back some Chinese refugees and other exploited people whom American soldiers had saved from certain extermi-nation in Mexico.

The catalogue of courses from any California university reveals the intellectual world that immigrants and their children can be press-ganged into. There are dozens of classes on Chicano pride, but scarcely any on the seminal events of American history. Recently I was looking at the list of classes from the University of California at Santa Barbara for the academic year 2001–2002. Sixty-two different courses were listed under "Chicano Studies," among them Introduction to Chicano Spanish; Methodology of the Oppressed; Barrio Popular Culture; Body, Culture, and Power; Chicana Feminism; History of the Chicano; History of the Chi-cano Movement; History of Chicano and Chicana Workers; Racism in American History; Chicano Political Organizing; Chi-cana Writers; De-colonizing Cyber-Cinema; Dance of the Chicanos; and dozens more. The history department offerings included thirteen similar courses on Latino and Chicano issues, in addition to more generic classes on race and oppression. But the entire catalogue had only one class on the Civil War per se, "Civil War and Reconstruction." There were no real courses dedicated to either the Revolutionary War or World War II.

What is truly fascinating about the ethnic pride courses is

that there has been no evolution in the subject matter over the three decades that such courses have been taught—even though there is now a growing third generation of one-quarter, one-half and full Hispanics who speak no Spanish and have never been to Mexico. Racism and oppression were de rigueur in the early 1970s, when racial studies departments and professorships were forced upon timid administrators. But why should racism and oppression remain as unchanged themes thirty years later, when Mexicans are no longer a minority of less than a million, but the largest ethnic group in the state of California and the largest minority in the nation? Could we not go down from sixty-two courses to perhaps ten? Aging La Raza professors, who drive their SUVs in from the suburbs and send their kids to UCLA and Berkeley, continue in some time warp to denigrate a system that has given them and their families so much.

The theory behind such a curriculum, of course, is that someone without competitive educational skills in English, the sciences and history might come to UC Santa Barbara or UC Davis and there regain a lost sense of self-esteem through "Methodology of the Oppressed." Or that armed with theoretical grievances, this student might be able to spot how the University of California—a metaphor for the wider world—in some ways sought to disenfranchise or otherwise exploit the Chicano student. Meanwhile, "white" students can also take such courses as a form of masochism to discover why they must become religiously devoted to bilingual education and affirmative action, and must make various sorts of reparation for past inequities—their contribution toward legitimizing the very race industry that offers such therapeutic courses in the first place.

Such institutionalized therapy is the sad legacy of the *Movimiento*—the great upheaval of the 1960s in which Mexican-American intellectual elites sought redress of past racism and stereotyping by the mandate of a pure racial identity and grand talk of ethnic separatism. The wages of this original sin are with us still—the idea that so-called Chicanos can find parity with whites only through government coercion, income redistribution and racial chauvinism, rather than by the very hard work of traditional education that once ensured that Mexican kids spoke perfect English, knew as much about math and science as members of any other ethnic group, and expected to find status and respect by becoming educated and prosperous.

In the pursuit of fashionable partial truths, the Truth was lost. Yes, most immigrants to the United States, not just Mexicans, were discriminated against. European Jews, the Irish, African slaves, the Japanese all had equal or worse horror stories. Millions of Mexicans, nevertheless, at great risk came to America rather than stay in Mexico because, like these other groups, they wanted a better life, and knew that millions of others under similar duress had achieved it. Because they slice history and culture so crookedly and because they are unable to deal with complex issues, poorly educated and politically biased intellectuals have tangled the entire Mexican immigrant community in a paradox: if America were so discriminatory and racist, and Mexico for its part such a wonderful society, why would any Mexican in this day of easy information flow ever come north to such a certified hell-hole?

Does anyone doubt that a resident alien from Mexico in her first year of college, should she enroll in Latin, classical studies and European history courses, might gain more knowledge of America's heritage and learn the basics of grammar and syntax in ways impossible in "Chicano Body, Culture, and Power"? Or better yet, would not a classics major of Mexican heritage gain more self-esteem through real achievement and mastery of literature than by picking up clichés and slogans from the 1960s recycled in today's "postcolonial" history classes?

If "white" California is to be blamed for anything, it is for creating fiefdoms for hundreds of professors in the race business to fabricate classes and methods of instruction that impart almost none of the useful cultural information desperately needed by an alien seeking to prosper in America. If there is truly a lingering racism in California, then one need go no further than the state universities, where so much money and power has been handed over to an elite class of racialists who in return have created a curriculum designed to guarantee failure for the children of migrants. The victim in all this really is the Chicano student—but the oppressor is his cynical university advocate, who uses him to advance an agenda that ensures only a comfortable academic existence, not a greater likelihood of completing college. So far, not one study has shown how a La Raza studies department has affected the tragedy that between 30 and 40 percent of all Hispanics won't graduate from high school. But the one thing that young Mexican-Americans, so woefully denied access to knowledge about much else, do learn is the nomenclature of the race industry and how to classify and reclassify themselves according to the label of the day: Hispanic, Latino, Chicano/Chicana, Mexicano, Mexican, Mexican-American, Mestizo, Latin American, Nuevomexicano, Californio, Tejano, and on and on.

Names change, programs come and go, but what stays constant is the same dismal graduation rates and thus the same overrepresentation of Mexicans and Mexican-Americans in our jails, prisons and welfare programs. I have a fantasy that somewhere in some secretive laboratory in Montana a white supremacist and a crackpot racist got together, brewed the germs of our present school curriculum, concocted the virus of the La Raza separatist and racist mythology, and then released these pathogens by night in aerosol form to be inhaled by unsuspecting Californians, who then proceeded unknowingly to destroy the aspirations of millions of desperately poor aliens.

Acting under the psychosis caused by such intellectual germ warfare, we institutionalized an easy bilingual education rather than implemented an intensive program of English instruction for immigrants. In the current atmosphere of relativism, who is to say, after all, that any nation needs a common language? Or that speaking grammatically and writing clearly, in English or even in Spanish, constitute education—especially when this age-old education comes at the expense of an indigenous language and culture, and thus purportedly threatens the self-esteem of a future doctor or lawyer of color?

The fervent advocacy of bilingual education on the part of Latino elites has been a baffling development. Determined that the burgeoning population of young Mexican-Americans will not go the way of other minority groups and eventually lose both their native language and their ethnic identity, they press ever forward with an agenda that deprives these immigrants of the fluency and expertise in English that the past assimilationist and immersionist models insisted upon. After thirty years of such agitation, and with ample proof that California's recent ending of most bilingualism in its schools has raised Latino test scores, it is now legitimate to question the very motives of some in the La Raza movement: do they wish the best for the children of aliens who are poor, or continued spoils for themselves who are affluent?

Again, we butt up against a tragic paradox: the young Chicano who visits the emergency room does not want to be treated by a doctor who cannot read and understand the rather complex directions on a vial of lifesaving antibiotic that are likely to be printed only in English. He hopes that his surgeon also understands English perfectly and grasps intricate printed warnings about the fatal interactions between various medicines. He expects—no, demands—that his Hispanic nurse be able to communicate effortlessly with the supervising physician in English as she measures out potentially deadly antitoxins. Even a Chicano-Latino professor, should he need kidney surgery, would probably confess that he hopes his urologist was an undergraduate biology or history major rather than the possessor of a Chicano studies degree.

Instead of offering immigrants the chance to strive for commonly recognized excellence, we tell them that the cultures they came from are all inherently equal—almost so as to deny the very reasons why these aliens arrived here in the first place. This message is cynical at its core, for we know that some other cultures and nations have been not merely different, but often far worse at providing freedom and security for their people. But to maintain the fiction of cultural equality, our schools, while harrowing up the evil in the soil of America, have waffled on the fifty million or more killed by Mao and Stalin, the existence of slavery in contemporary Sudan, and the rampant corruption and lawlessness in Mexico today. In this regard, American schools have also completely failed to note the critical distinction between a multiracial and a multicultural society. The former welcomes all races to learn one language and heritage; such a society is found only in the present-day West. The latter encourages separate but purportedly equal languages and traditions, and is a prescription for disaster—as we have seen in Bosnia, Rwanda, Sudan, Somalia and much of India.

Serving side dishes of therapeutic history and imagery to each racial and ethnic group, an idea hatched in the 1970s, not only erodes the basis of national unity, but also emboldens the architects of separatism to demand even more concessions from appeasers in the deans' offices and legislatures. Suddenly we had racial enclaves throughout the university, segregated "theme" houses and graduation ceremonies, the institutionalization of racist assumptions, and set-asides in university admissions. Concessions denoted weakness, which was felt to be evidence of guilt arising over past prejudice, and that, in turn, justified more present concessions.

Almost all of our university research into issues of health, the environment and crime has become astonishingly separatist, and the racially charged ideas peddled in thousands of master's and doctoral theses have trickled down into our daily papers, to be digested by the general public. In one week alone, I read in our local newspaper the following five stories:

First, a "recent study" suggested that Hispanics were forced to breathe worse air than Anglos. The method of arriving at such a finding was never discussed, but apparently we were to imagine that power plants or polluting industries were deliberately placed in barrios. Am I supposed to believe that the bad air that I and thousands of white others breathe in the Central Valley is any different from what my Mexican neighbor three hundred yards away inhales? Does toxic air simply hover in one place while people stay put to breathe it in? Does Parlier, which is 99 percent Hispanic, have dark clouds of particulate matter while five miles away the town of Reedley, which is more white than Mexican-American, enjoys clear blue skies?

The next story reported that diabetes was more common among Mexican people after they arrived in the United States than it had been in Mexico—a result of their partaking in our malignant diet. Such an unfortunate statistic may be true. But the article's author teased out a further implication: that cheap American fast food, through nefarious corporate advertising, had been foisted particularly upon people of color and was contributing in a racist fashion to their premature deaths. Nowhere in the story was there an acknowledgment that Mexicans, like everyone else, must educate themselves as to the value of fruits and vegetables, and strive to avoid Coca Cola, beer, Big Macs and fries, with Twinkies for dessert. The article gave no statistics on diabetes and obesity among poor white people—a group that seems to have been no more successful in avoiding such lethally starchy, high-fat diets. Nor did it acknowledge that such unwholesome fare, while certainly unfavorable to well-being and longevity, might be safer in the short term than many of the foods and the water in rural Mexico that are laced with bacteria and parasites. Thus while Mexican aliens are perhaps becoming obese, they are now suffering far less from catastrophic dysenteries and malnutrition—and therefore, on the whole, living longer in America than they would in rural Mexico.

The third newspaper article, in advocating more medical interpreters for Mexican patients, alleged that local doctors on average spent far less time with Hispanics than with their white counterparts. Again, the methodology was never exactly specified. (What constituted "Hispanic"—one-quarter, one-half, three-quarters Mexican ancestry? Who and how many doctors or patients were interviewed and what were they asked?) But more importantly, the journalists did not address three or four obvious though unpleasant questions: Why should American doctors hire interpreters for patients *inside America?* Why does the Hispanic community not insist on more English immersion programs to ensure that the sick are able to communicate effectively and at length with their doctors? Why do not children or relatives who speak English interpret for patients instead of costly state translators? And finally, is this a distinctly American problem? Would the Mexican government worry much that Americans in Mexico did not understand Spanish—and therefore got shorter shrift from doctors—when they visited Mexican hospitals?

A fourth newspaper report alleged that more Mexicans than whites have been jailed under California's somewhat draconian "Three Strikes and You're Out" legislation. Again, the obvious question was never raised: Could it be because they were committing more third strikes than their white or Asian counterparts—and if so, why? Nor did the article wonder: If Mexicans were going to prison in large numbers for committing felonies such as murder, rape, theft and assault, who were their victims? Could it be mainly innocent Mexicans? The account also did not raise other issues such as whether Mexicans committed proportionally more violent crimes against Anglos than Anglos against Mexicans.

The final pertinent story I encountered in my week's reading centered on a number of aliens who have tragically died in the Arizona desert. The main theme of the article was that California's recent "fence" near San Diego and its increased border vigilance there, coupled with the American "paranoia" after 9/11, had caused dozens of poor immigrants to die of dehydration along the much more perilous and poorly demarcated routes through the desert. The reader was to conclude that overt racism had resulted in a policy to kill innocent Mexicans who simply wished to come to the Untied States to better themselves. The obvious logical counterarguments were absent from the story. Why did a fence arise in the first place south of San Diego, if not to stop thousands of Mexicans from simply storming through immigration control and onto the streets and highways of southern California, endangering themselves and startled motorists? Did a nation that recently lost three thousand of its citizens to foreign terrorists, some of whom were here illegally, not have the right to police its own borders? Did the Mexican government have culpability for the tragedy in the Arizona desert by not bothering to keep its citizenry from coming north under such radically changed conditions? And when the United States decided that in a time of war it wished to reinforce its border policies, should it have made illegal border-crossing much more difficult or only a little bit more difficult?

The "progressive" worldview that churns out such stories has completely lost the sense of human precariousness common to all civilizations. Rather than confess that mankind by its very nature is prone to be murderous, sexist and racist—and that only liberal institutions of the West can rein in these innate proclivities—we instead demand instantaneous perfection of our own country and no other, both in the present and in the past. Nowhere in these stories is there any allowance for human fallibility or weakness, no admission that Twinkies can be more alluring to the palate than cabbage, or that doctors, fearing constant lawsuits and increasingly employed as bureaucrats by HMOs, naturally feel better able to relate to people who speak their own language.

Worse still, the constant refrain that "they" are doing such terrible things to Hispanics perpetuates the myth that what one selects to eat, what language one chooses to learn, what crime one commits or forgoes—all that and more is beyond the realm of individual agency and rather subject to larger deterministic forces, usually prejudicial in nature.

Sometimes the problem is not so much the slanted ideology of such popular news accounts, but simply the imbalance that is a part of basic reporting today. What constitutes real news now? Take, for example, a typical issue of the *Fresno Bee*, this one dated Monday, November 25, 2002. Greater Fresno and the surrounding sprawl are now a considerable metropolis of nearly one million people—a large city more than a rural backwater. And November 2002 was a perilous time in American history, as the United States began to ponder war with Iraq while continuing to wage a multi-pronged campaign against terrorists. Yet nobody would suspect any of that from reading the front page of the city newspaper. The top headline blared, "Man Slain After Chase Ends Near Selma," over an article detailing how a young Hispanic criminal confronted law enforcement officials after a carjacking, threatened to kill them, and then was gunned down not far from where I live.

The next story on the right, headlined "Donations to Mexico Stranded," explained how efforts by local Hispanics to send food and clothing to the Mexican town of Nayarit after the devastations of Hurricane Kenna had been stymied by the inefficiency and obduracy of the Mexican consulate. The care packages were still sitting on pallets in a Fresno warehouse weeks after the disaster. The third headline, on the left side of the front page, announced that "Fresno's Motel Kids Find New Digs," and the story chronicled new efforts to house foster children.

At the bottom of the page, "Young Migrants Follow Perilous Path North" presented the theme that very young Mexicans are crossing illegally on their own and not being treated very well by smugglers. The story suggested that their harsh experiences were somehow the fault of the United States because of a failure to enact a new border agreement with Mexico. One illegal alien in Georgia was quoted as reassuring her underage son, who had been sent back across the border, not to worry because she would employ the smuggler to try again to lead him across the desert.

Still searching for a story about world affairs this November morning—was there anything going on besides unfair treatment of local Hispanics?—I turned to the editorial page. There were three opinion essays. At the top was a column by Roberto Rodriquez entitled "Exceptions to 'All Life Is Sacred' Tough to Reconcile." Rodriquez faulted the hypocrisy of anti-abortion activists for supporting the death penalty (but not pro-abortion activists for opposing it) and detailed how such insight about the preciousness

of life was inculcated in him by Mexican elders when he was growing up in Tijuana and had an irrational fear of ants. The logic in
the rambling and incoherent piece was hard to follow as it skipped
between the death penalty, Mexico, abortion, bombing and ant
colonies, but somehow I gathered that an older generation of Mexicans had taught Rodriquez about a superior way of viewing life
on earth, and that we as Americans should follow his creed so that
we don't go to war to "crush them like ants" and kill "tens of
thousands of innocent civilians." Inasmuch as I had just read on
page one that some Mexican parents were sending their own
twelve-year-old children unescorted across the scorching Arizona
desert in violation of American law, and that the Mexican government was abetting such a dangerous trek, and that Mr. Rodriquez
had obviously abandoned his beloved Mexico for a callous United
States, I was confused by his invective.

Ruben Navarrete Jr. wrote the second essay, right below the
Rodriquez piece: "Ethnic Hyphen Symbol of Pride, Not Separatism." In it he argued that using hyphenated self-identification
was hardly antithetical to national unity. This also troubled me
inasmuch as the usually sensible Mr. Navarrete grew up near me
with middle-class parents, had little if any contact with either
Mexico or recent immigrants, and does not speak Spanish. His call
for people like himself to self-identify as Mexican-American
would be as useful as my adopting the label "Swedish-American"
when I do not speak Swedish, do not live among Swedish immigrants, and know nothing of life in Sweden. The only reason for
me to identify myself in that way would be to invest in some sort
of movement or ideology that brought real attention to or preferences for Swedish-Americans.

The third op-ed, at the bottom of the page, was by George
Will on the future political makeup of the U.S. Senate.

And all that was what passed for a day's headlines and commentary for the hundreds of thousands of readers in the central San
Joaquin Valley. The tragedy here lay not merely in the marked imbalance of the *Fresno Bee*'s efforts to reach new readers, but in its

condescending approach to Americans of Mexican descent. The assumption was that they would naturally rather read about the daily hometown shootouts, the pride of hyphenated IDs or even ants in Tijuana than about whether their own country was going to war.

If we were ultimately to trace the DNA of such stories in the popular media or explain the obsession with race and separatism, we must look to the avalanche of books from Latino studies departments across the United States. As a single but representative example, take the recent anthology entitled *Latinos: Remaking America* (California, 2002), edited by M. Suárez-Orozco and M. Páez, a professor and a researcher at Harvard, and subsidized by the David Rockefeller Center for Latin American Studies. The two scholars collect twenty-one essays whose general theme seems to be that racism, the brutalities of American capitalism, right-wing reaction and general neglect by white people have all conspired to hold Latinos back in America. Forget for the moment the irony of such attacks on the system being published through icons of American capitalism like David Rockefeller, the endowment of Harvard University, and the state-subsidized University of California Press; instead, examine the lengths to which the book's authors go to explain away any positive developments on the immigration front.

The first essay sees intermarriage in a bad light. ("But investing that sort of utopian power in the genetic mixing of our era only serves to heighten a new form of racial essentialism and once again to frame the process of overcoming racial hierarchy as a fundamentally biological one.") A book devoted to race is now worried that "mixing" (the phrase itself has echoes of "mongrelization") might make race irrelevant and dilute racial power along with bloodlines.

Another essay in the book struggles with the fact that Cubans were given over $1 billion in the decade between 1965 and 1976 by the federal government to aid in refugee resettlement, and that the recipients were mostly whiter, wealthier and more conservative

Latinos. Confronted with these bothersome facts demonstrating American generosity, communist persecution, and dramatic success in the United States, the author hopes that refugees from Central and South America who are poor and dark-skinned will dilute this Cuban strength, prevent more embarrassing scenes like the Elián Gonzalez demonstration, and end the "hegemony" of Miami's' Cuban elite and their "fixation" on Castro.

The next essay criticizes rude "Anglo teachers who reprimanded Mexican students for speaking Spanish," along with the cruelty of free markets ("rapid industrialization and capitalist development"), as being instrumental in creating barrio gangs. Somehow it is capitalism that, after luring the oppressed across the border, keeps them perennially poor—a thesis that does not explain why it is that while Cubans of their own volition seek Florida, North Koreans go south and Mexicans trek north, the opposite is never the case.

Most of the book's twenty-one essays—which I can imagine being required reading for the future reporters of the *Fresno Bee* and other papers—struggle with the dilemma of proving racial prejudice when interracial marriage is at an all-time high. They posit blanket discrimination against Latinos, when Cubans are excelling in all areas of American society. They argue that a recent rise in test scores following the demise of bilingual education means nothing if it jeopardizes the power of the mother tongue, and insist that affirmative action must remain based on race rather than poverty despite an emergent Hispanic middle class. After being exposed to such professors, their programs and their books, an innocent would have to assume that the progress of Hispanics in America is a dispiriting failure. Someone not so innocent would understand that the chief fears of such intellectuals are no longer racial prejudice, but rather the end of the primacy of race, and the dissolution of minority blocs in voting, residence and mindset.

The new race industry is not restricted to Ph.D.s in the universities. On the local level, hundreds of teachers, government bureaucrats and union officials are committed to the same agenda of separatism and racial spoils. And given the sheer numbers of new immigrants, the undeniable past history of racism in California, the trendy guilt of the California suburbanite, and the failure of all too many Mexican immigrants to find economic success commensurate with that enjoyed by Koreans, Punjabis and other new arrivals, we do live in a time of an unusual opportunity for the demagogue and provocateur. Let me be clear on this: the race-hustler is *not* at one with the millions of successful third- and fourth-generation Hispanics in California who pretty much go to work and tune him out, and whose own race is rather low on their list of pressing issues, far behind the next raise, the struggle against backyard rye grass, and the choice between an all-terrain Jeep or a minivan. It is also true that the type of the brawling race provocateur is as old as America itself. In some sense, he is related to the Irish ward boss, the Polish precinct worker and the Italian borough master of former times. A century out of date, he shares a nineteenth-century vision of enormous ethnic blocks, entirely unassimilated, with tough burly capos like himself riding to prominence at their head. He imagines himself as bursting into locked rooms, bowling over the timid man at the podium, and wresting out entitlements and quotas for his clients based on their percentages in the nation's population.

This racialist is akin to the union organizer of a past era—but now government money rather than wages, now reparations and entitlements rather than mere patronage are his requisition. He knows where and when to press his demand: now to bully the meek college president; now to be more cautious in the push for quotas and entitlements at the less pleasant arena of farm, construction site or food plant, with tougher pink folk of tattoos and missing teeth.

The chief fear of the race manipulator? That unchecked immigration may cease; that his minions may learn to read and write English with ease; that his brother or sister may marry "the other"; that a Mexican middle class might flourish in private enterprise apart from government service or entitlements; that the Mexican propensity for duty, family and self-sacrifice might yet take hold in the United States and make him obsolete.

Sometimes in the murky world of affirmative action, the activist turns out not really to be Mexican at all, but Chilean, Basque or Spanish! Indeed, we at the university regularly hire those from abroad with Hispanic last names to ensure that we are seen as a "diverse" community. (Part of the genius of the postmodern term "Hispanic" is that it gives quite a lot of cover for well-heeled Europeans and South Americans to receive preferences over native-born Americans.) The racialist may also be the well-meaning but Spanish-illiterate Latino weekend anchorman, who suddenly changes his name from John to Juan and never meets another "r" he won't trill. In the new media patois, local Hispanic politicians and judges in the news become "Hooseee Gonzzaleees," while murderers and rapists who appear on the screen are merely "Joe Gonzales."

The professional Latino means well, but his passion is not put in the service of racial or ethnic harmony, much less the truth. He is a professed tribalist of the first order who does *not* wish to live within his tribe. He has little desire to help his brethren by promoting the kind of assimilative culture that he simultaneously critiques and wants, and knows is his only salvation if his car, house and job title are any indication. He may make speeches and films about gang violence and teen pregnancy, but he never really tells us why these phenomena are widespread among "his people" or how they can be prevented. It is so much easier to leave cause and effect unacknowledged, so much more lucrative to sprinkle racism and victimization as cheap condiments here and there in his public rounds.

In this context, it is hard not to have grim thoughts about the white, liberal, guilty and frightened college presidents of the past few decades who set up racial satrapies on California campuses. Now safely retired in California coastal or mountain retreats, they have left behind a legacy of absurd intellectual ghettoes whose inhabitants are always angry. March once on the president's office in the 1960s and acquire a Chicano studies professorship; march twice and gain an entire ward, replete with separate theme dorms and private graduation ceremonies. After all, if in their private lives such white men preferred to live only among other affluent white people, why at work wouldn't they approve of separate dorms, departments and graduations for brown people?

Few of the Mexican-American friends I grew up with in my home-town speak fluent Spanish anymore, whether or not they finished college. (Completing eighth grade then provided a far better education than finishing high school does now.) They may not all be titled and degreed, but almost all are informed and can read, write, compute and understand the basic tenets of the culture they have helped to build and maintain—and which they most certainly think is far superior to that of Mexico. Their children know only a few words of Spanish—quite in contrast to the present 65 percent of all foreign-born Hispanics in the United States, who now speak only limited English. Most of my generation have become insurance salesmen, mechanics, contractors, teachers, civil servants, occasionally wealthy businessmen and high government officials—in other words, the present-day "future of California." There are no Mexican flags on their cars, which more likely sport decals like "Proud Parent of a Lincoln School Honor Student" or "*Semper Fi.*" About half of them, it seems to me, are not married to Mexican-Americans.

Most vote as Democrats, but are probably anti-abortion and perhaps even support the death penalty. Some joined and prospered in the Marines; others run the Lions and Kiwanis clubs. They are sensitive to occasional news of prejudice, yet display little affinity for the race-and-ethnicity industry that has taken hold on the CSU campus at nearby Fresno. In their daily lives, they are more worried about gangs and Mexican crime than about white racism. A few seem conscious of race, but only when the father is Anglo, the mother Mexican. This is because affirmative action (whether now legal or not), they believe, is not so affirmative toward a Justin Smith who is half Mexican as to a Justin Martinez or even the suspect Justin Smith-Martinez, although each is Mexican in the same measure.

But perhaps the well-integrated middle-age and middle-class residents of Selma are an exception and belong to an age gone by. For the most part, the children of illegal aliens not only are not learning the skills to compete with native-born Americans; they also in frustration are receptive to the lure of ethnic chauvinism— constantly promoted by their teachers—to treat their wounded pride. In surveys conducted by the Russell Sage Foundation from the mid-1990s, children of immigrants were shown to have doggedly resisted assimilation. Five thousand students were surveyed at 13 years of age and then again at 17 to inquire about their attitudes toward their adopted country. Even after—or perhaps because of—four years of enrollment in American high schools, they were 50 percent more likely to identify themselves as "Mexican" or "Filipino" than as "Mexican-American" or "Filipino-American." So we can at least be sure that efforts to instill ethnic pride have two indisputable effects: they create a sense that the children of immigrants are not even what Theodore Roosevelt referred to as "hyphenated Americans," and ensure that they will not be given the rigorous training that allows them to compete on a level playing field. Indeed, the two phenomena are inextricably connected: the more the Chicano student takes therapeutic classes, the more he senses his own failure to achieve parity with other Americans, and the more he falls back on ethnic pride to supply the confidence he cannot acquire through intellectual achievement—and finally, the more his teachers, who themselves either cannot or will not instruct, must push the elixir of ethnic identification.

California has always been a great, though risky experiment in a truly multiracial society, united by a common language, culture and law—something not seen since the creation of the Roman Principate, in which *Pax Romana* was to give—or else!—the Gaul, the Spaniard and the Thracian alike the Italian notions of government, water via aqueduct, Juvenal's *Satires* and habeas corpus. But that subjugation of race to culture is forever a fragile state, not a natural condition. Each day it erodes if not actively maintained. Race, chauvinism, ethnicity creep hourly back into social life if not battled by citizens of strength and vision. A few malicious people can undo the work of centuries. Thus, each time a university president, a small-time politician on the make, or a *bien pensant* liberal journalist chooses the easy path of separatism, he does a little part in turning us toward Rwanda or Yugoslavia. The work of cultural unity is of the ages; advancing racial and ethnic separatism is a gesture of the moment.

How, then, can we recreate civic education to help unite an increasingly fragmented society, and to bring Hispanics and other recent arrivals into the body politic of the United States? It will not be easy—if only because millions of Americans in education, the arts and government have invested a great deal in, and profited handsomely from, a relativist and multicultural society that rejects any unifying core. Their dream is vastly different from the multiracial society in which millions of Americans with a broad spectrum of skin colors speak the same English, share the same commitment to the values of the Constitution, and gradually become indistinguishable through integration, assimilation and intermarriage. Returning to a multiracial society under the aegis of Western culture would put a lot of people in the universities, politics and government bureaucracies quite literally out of business.

What, then, can we do? We must reject the new cultural relativism, situational ethics and arrogant utopianism that have escaped from the university and circulate like an airborne toxin in the popular culture. Scholars must stop teaching nonsense like the idea that Harriet Tubman and Sojourner Truth, important though they were, affected American history more profoundly than John Adams or Alexander Hamilton, or that gangsta rap is essentially no less musical than Beethoven. Rather than blame the United States for persistent imperfection, our educators should emphasize how far we have come in eradicating sins that seem intractable to much of humankind elsewhere.

Just as importantly, we should acknowledge that the new vocationalism of the Right is as pernicious as the multiculturalism of the Left. If students are taught that the main purpose of education is to impart lucrative skills—profitable business acumen or accounting expertise—and that the accompanying good life will itself constitute the Good Life, it will be impossible to mold a generation that will welcome sacrifice or develop any common concern about the well-being of the less fortunate.

Rarely do our students ever learn anything about the great American Captains—Washington, Winfield Scott, Sherman, Grant, Pershing, Patton, Bradley, Doolittle—either because of a general dogma that war is always evil and unnecessary, or simply because of the military ignorance of their teachers. Yet no society can long survive if it cannot produce men of war who emerge in its darkest hours to defend, without subverting, its most cherished values. Caesar Chavez and Susan B. Anthony—whose names all of today's grade-school students seem to recognize—may have been great reformers, but there simply would not have been anything to reform if not for people such as Grant, Sherman and Patton, whose genius and achievements are part of our youth's vast historical illiteracy.

My own elementary school is still two miles away, but whereas forty years ago it turned out skilled and confident Americans, its graduates who enter high school now have among the lowest literacy levels and the most dismal math skills in the state. The lucky ones who eventually go on to college are likely to be among the 47 percent of students entering the California State University system who need remedial classes—the largest university in the world, and *nearly half the freshmen take high-school, not college, courses.*

Yet for Hispanics, just reaching the remedial CSU programs

is a great achievement in itself. Despite millions in federal and state expenditures in the last twenty years, by 1996 only 61 percent of Hispanics—both native and foreign-born—had graduated from high school. Nearly a decade later, out of every 100 Hispanics—native or foreign-born, illegal or lawful immigrants, citizens or aliens—who now enter California high schools, *30 will drop out.* And of the remaining 70, fewer than 4 will matriculate prepared for any serious college-level courses in mathematics. Less than 10 percent of all adult Mexican-Americans currently hold a bachelor's degree.

Some may argue over the data, wondering precisely who are those listed as "Hispanic" on surveys and by what chronological parameters a failure to graduate is measured. And new data in the twenty-first century may shed a different light on all this. But what is unarguable is that we are clearly faced with skyrocketing asymmetries between Hispanic and non-Hispanic performance in our schools—a problem that has been apparent since the 1970s, when hundreds of thousands of aliens began coming into this country illegally and were adopted by the intellectual inheritors of the prior decade's political radicalism.

How then did we get to this present dilemma in California? How did we arrive at a world where thousands of citizens have lounged, embittered, on the dole while harvests go unpicked? How did we ignore thousands here, but demand that thousands more come illegally from across the border? How did we manufacture provocateurs at the university who burn the flag of the land they so desperately want to inhabit, while they proudly wave the flag of the country they so demonstrably prefer to abandon? How did we craft a society where the juvenile chooses the barbarism of the predatory jungle, but when injured or maimed he emerges from the wild to demand as his inalienable right the expensive succor of a compassionate and ordered culture he professes to despise? How did we create an intelligentsia that offers as models the despot Montezuma and the outlaw Pancho Villa, instead of Socrates and Lincoln?

If Mexico had not been contiguous to the United States, *if* migrants had only come in the thousands, not millions, *if* self-proclaimed advocates on campus and in the media had been honest and responsible folk, and *if* this had remained an America of the melting pot rather than the separatist culture of the 1980s and 1990s, then, I think, we would have fewer problems with race, culture and immigration.

But that is a lot of ifs.

SIX
A Remedy in Popular Culture?

WE MUST KEEP SOME PERSPECTIVE. Even if only six out of ten California residents of Mexican heritage are really graduating from high school, that figure still implies that every year, hundreds of thousands of Mexicans and Mexican-Americans are entering the work force in occupations other than menial labor and slowly finding their way into the mainstream, to join earlier immigrants in the American middle and upper classes.

It is not uncommon in my hometown to be stopped by a Mexican-American policeman, to talk about one's kids with a Mexican-American school principal, and to remonstrate with a Mexican-American city council member—many of them identifiable as being of Mexican heritage only by surname, never by accent, manner or appearance. Small business men and women—restaurant owners, brake shop owners, labor contractors and truck fleet owners—are increasingly Mexican-Americans.

What this progress proves is that millions of Mexican aliens and their offspring grew up in California at a time when high standards and civic education were still embedded within the public schools and when assimilation, not separatism or multiculturalism, was the model of success. In contrast, the legions of more recently arrived Mexicans and the youth who grew up in the very different environment of the 1980s and 1990s have not had these benefits, and are now stranded in a destructive in-betweenness, often the pawns of those who play the parlor game of identity politics.

Yet for all the harm done to Mexican immigrants by both the naïve and the opportunistic, there is nevertheless another, countervailing engine of change at work in America. It is the more nebulous and wholly amoral power of a new popular and global culture, whose intrinsic character is to unite us all in shared appetites for material things that dissolve the old prejudices of race, class, language and culture. In 1960 a Mexican immigrant student was taught the positives of the United States in his classes and told to emulate his peers through rapid acceptance of American culture—even as he found his Anglo girlfriend's parents wary, the new music and customs foreign, personal discrimination undeniable, and formalities at work and play constant reminders of his otherness. Now the opposite is true: the schools and government seek to accentuate his differences—even as he wades knee-deep into a world that doesn't much care whom he dates, and where he feels at home with the prevailing, and already familiar, tastes in music, clothes and television.

Is globalization like the dark, godless power of Tolkien's ring—or is it the calmer, more uniform and postheroic world after the destruction of that ring, where uniqueness and difference vanish without the need of elemental struggles along age-old divides of culture and politics? I resent the cultural obliteration caused by global uniformity—which is wiping out our small farm along with the community of which I was a part—but I am not so naïve as to deny that ultimately, and perhaps by accident, its results are radically homogenizing, leveling, and so in a weird sense democratic at the most basic, popular level. I may find the new Selma crass and boring, and may prefer the old—but I accept that most would not agree and would rightfully claim that life at the material level is far easier today and far more informal.

The new residents of Selma would find my old nostalgic world of small-town America—farmers exchanging pleasantries in little shops and family businesses—static, hierarchical, exclusionary and far more repressive, impoverished and boring than the wide-open society of our new malls. That Selma as I once knew it is dead; yet its obituary for most Mexican-Americans comes as good news, not bad, for its successor edge city on the freeway offers opportunity and comfort undreamed of a half-century ago. Before, when we purchased a car, we went to see Ed Butler and his single salesman over at the Ford agency, listened to an hour-long talk about raisin prices and Sun-Maid inefficiency, perused his glossy "catalog" to inquire about ordering extras like seat belts and radios, and handed him a check for a down payment on delivery in six weeks (or, as in the case of my nineteenth-century grandfather, paid cash carefully withdrawn from a savings account). Now we all go to the sprawling, multimillion-dollar Auto-Mall, with its inventory of five thousand autos, and can walk out with a $40,000 SUV on a Visa card.

Globalization and its harmonious bastard culture will put out to pasture the race agitator at the university, but it may well also drown out beautiful Mexican folk songs with American-style rock in Spanish. Sounds of hip-hop draw blonds and Koreans alike. Television assumes interracial smooching. Gay desire makes no distinction between brown and black, who fight alike the sexual prejudices of their respective cultures.

Celebrity magazines with glossy pictures and little text proliferate, aimed at the illiterate of all races. Bestsellers are often confined to mystery, sex and diet—with plenty of illustrations, big fonts and a vocabulary of fewer than a thousand words, all readable in a couple of hours. The current taste in popular music runs to shouting laced with obscenity, underscored by a pounding, totalitarian rhythm. These assaults on formality, prior erudition, modesty and manners may be offensive, but they assume that almost all Americans, without education or knowledge of fixed genres, find instant commonality with one another through the medium of desire.

The supercharged nature of such texts, pictures and sounds, delivered instantaneously through inexpensive radios, televisions

and the Internet—along with the swift and easy way they are discussed and debated via cell phones and e-mail—has the effect of
creating a dynamic popular ethos that often trumps all previous
hierarchies. Not only are the authority of family, religion and government waning, but all the suppositions and pretensions of the
old culture—class considerations, racial prejudices, snobbery of
any sort—are silenced as well by the high-decibel magnetism of
popular entertainment and its ferocious dumbing-down to the
level of easiest comprehension and acceptance. What a war the
new popular culture has inadvertently taken up through the pursuit of its own naked greed—no less than an assault on the age-old
class, race and gender hierarchies that were previously thought to
be innate to, and unassailable within, the human condition!

Globalization can now unite any two people from the most
disparate backgrounds in taste, appearance and manner of daily
life. Humberto Gama, who lives down the road from me, has been
in the United States for twenty years. I am not sure of his legal
status, a topic never broached between us. He works occasional
jobs—farm work and construction mostly—and is married with
three children. I still hear only Spanish waft across the vineyard
from his numerous parties and weekend festivities. He has filed for
workman's compensation, been on welfare, received unemployment
insurance—and worked on and off the entire time he has been
drawing his various subsidies; a global citizen, he assumes that the
spreading Western idea of entitlement can ameliorate the occasional roughness of the marketplace. I have little idea what he
makes, but imagine it is under $30,000. He drives a 1991 Chevy
Astro van, which he bought used for about $3,000. It looks not
all that different from a $30,000 new model, and for purposes of
driving to town and back, it is just as serviceable. His sneakers,
jeans, T-shirts and hat—off the rack from Kmart, Old Navy and
The Gap—look no different from mine. He has no health insurance, but then various state and federal programs and local clinics
seem to provide him with adequate care. To my knowledge he has
never forgone medical treatment for lack of funds, and he doesn't

worry much about the pro forma bills that occasionally come from the Selma hospital—an institution claiming to be millions of dollars in the red each fiscal year. We forget that globalization is not merely the proliferation of goods, but also of notions of entitlement, and Humberto at least expects high-tech medical care as part of his newfound affluence.

People in town treat him no differently from me. In the new classless society of California, the fact that I have a Ph.D. in classics and he quit high school somewhere in Mexico during his second year, while critical factors in determining our respective incomes, is mostly irrelevant. The status provided by educational attainment means absolutely nothing to people at McDonald's or Jiffy Lube, and perhaps even to the teachers we both encounter at the local back-to-school night. When I take my daughter to the emergency room with a bloody leg, we are given service no more quickly than is Humberto; health insurance cards, five generations of residence in the same town, ample capital, the ability to discuss with the physician the nature of the epidermis—all that and more means hardly a thing to the Hispanic clerk at the admittance window, and even less to the interns who put us way at the back of the line of wounded and ill in our brave new society.

This is all as it should be, but nevertheless is a revolutionary development in the history of civilization. Americans are actually the radical society that French intellectuals envisioned when they shook their fists at the barricades, before slinking back to their lounges and salons for more table talk and pipe dreams.

As neighbors, Humberto and I talk with a familiarity that suggests we are in the same class, have the same tastes and share similar problems. This is fact, not supposition, and the equality is natural, not forced. His television is nicer than mine; indeed, his family uses two cell phones. Their home—a small wooden ranch house—is provided by a local farmer to ensure his presence for occasional chores. Humberto listens to rap music on his work truck—a 1992 Dodge Dakota he bought from me in 1998 for $2,000 (paid over three months) with 80,000 miles on it. On purchase, he immediately put in a bed liner, added a new stereo, had it detailed—so now it is in better shape and more reliable than the Mazda I got to replace it, which has cost me much more in the last four years than Humberto's Dakota has cost him. And his teenagers, not mine, will be sent letters of invitation by a University of California desperate for "diversity," which they define largely by race. So is Mr. Gama poor and oppressed?

In terms of opportunity to travel, yes. He rarely ventures out of Fresno County. He eats out at Denny's, not an upscale restaurant in Fresno. He gulps down Snickers and Korn-Nuts, not Odwalla fruit drinks and celery sticks. Even at forty he is heavy, and not always well. His chances to find lucrative and steady employment are dwindling as his belly enlarges, his knees weaken and his English remains poor. Yet if one were to judge only by his clothes, the superficial appearance of his cars and appurtenances, or those of his wife and children—not to mention their consumer habits, their choice of entertainment and general tastes—the Gamas are not much different from the family of a third-generation California suburbanite who works for a software company for $100,000 a year.

Federal and state largess without stern audit, access to cheap consumer products imported from abroad, and a vast social network of friends and relatives have ensured that Humberto is royalty compared with his relatives back in Mexico. And there is, of course, the tax code. Humberto pays no tax on his off-the-books earnings, and almost no levies on his reported income. When I was growing up in Selma, we all paid income taxes; now those like Humberto who make below $30,000 pay almost none. In 1955 the military got 62 percent of all federal dollars, entitlements 21 percent; now this is reversed: individuals receive 61 percent of federal dollars and the military 17 percent. And this revolutionary notion that government is to rectify what individuals cannot has had dramatic effects in Selma. Welfare, disability, workman's compensation, Head Start, Social Security, Medicare, Medicaid, supplemental assistance—all that largess (and the avail-

ability of cheap Chinese-produced goods) has created a real consumer class from the immigrant community, the unemployed and
the half-employed—while this newfound affluence has made them,
in a way, angrier that they are still not as wealthy as others.

In short, Humberto Gama is outwardly indistinguishable
from many of the professors I work with. His car on its daily trek
into Selma looks not much different from those of soccer moms
on their way to upscale white suburban schools. Humberto's is a
Potemkin middle-class existence to be sure, but even its façade
simply did not exist a mere two decades ago, when I could easily
spot the clothes, cars, habits and general look of the illegal alien in
a matter of seconds. Now these distinguishing marks have been
dissolved by the advent of a globalized look, a veneer of sameness
and fraternity, an equal access to the electronic world of imagery
and message and the means to pay for it—with little regard for
actual earned income or racial identification.

This instant American satisfaction of the baser cravings has
enraged our European friends, who among their own youth see Big
Macs displacing haute cuisine, rap eclipsing more sophisticated
music, and *Star Wars* trouncing grim Swedish melodrama. Our liberal professors and journalists at home might enjoy the nuance and
minutes-long still shots of French film, but young whites from
Montana and Chicanos from East Los Angeles, if they watch foreign movies at all, alike prefer Jackie Chan. Immigrants from
Mexico tend to agree with the latter, not the former. They understand that American mores and tastes in the culture at large set few
requirements for full participation—not money, education, breeding, parentage, race, accent or religion. The Mexican immigrants
I know who listen to English-speaking radio are more likely to
turn to the loud and sometimes grating voices of Rush Limbaugh
or Michael Savage than to the subdued and often nasal tones
of NPR.

Almost anyone can understand the plot of an American
movie and sit transfixed by the human and technological pyrotech-
nics—car chases, explosions, murderous heroes on a mission of

revenge, bodies littered about, nudity, obscenity, sex scenes, syrupy endings. Video games, unlike books, plays or board games, are universally hypnotic precisely because they demand little literacy, provide explosions of color and imagery, and require only a type of eye-hand-brain synergy that is not culturally specific. Fast food offends few since it is neither spicy nor sour, and thus calls for no acquired taste. Instead it grows increasingly bland, ample and cheap—and packaged in such a way that it is as easily edible in a car as at a table.

Americans are criticized for preferring quicker, cheaper Taco Bell to more conventional and tastier real Mexican dishes; but then, illegal aliens too—especially young males—increasingly buy such American take-out rather than traditionally prepared tortillas. Their girlfriends agree, and—costs being about equal—likewise choose to eat in the car en route to the mall, rather than stay home in a hot kitchen rolling corn-flour dough. Mass communication through darting images on television, pictures on computer screens and photos in printed matter are more easily digested than written texts.

If such schlock is sweeping the globe—and along with it American English, American business protocols, American sports, American advertising, American media and American casual behavior—one can imagine the net effect of it all at its place of birth in America, of which California remains the epicenter. At a time when illegal immigration is at an all-time high, and formal efforts at forging a common culture and encouraging assimilation are at an all-time low, the habits, tastes, appetites and expressions of everyday people have offered a rescue of sorts—perhaps deleterious to the long-term moral health of the United States, but in the short term about the only tool we possess to prevent racial separation and ethnic tribalism. Informality in dress, slang speech, movies, videos, television—all this makes assimilation easier, even at a time when professional racialists are calling for highbrow separatism.

Critics—mostly affluent and highly educated—complain

that televised Monday night football, faked wrestling, 350 cable channels, nonstop coverage of Monica Lewinsky's antics or the tragedy of Chandra Levy all erode and cheapen our society. They suggest that we now predictably prefer the ephemeral to the lasting, and so care little anymore about good poetry, classical music, ballet, contemporary art, or even the fellowship of small farms, businesses and community get-togethers. And they are, of course, right. The kind of stable and uplifting culture that demands knowledge, training, education or familiarity for inclusion now thrives only in small enclaves in our major cities and some rural oases.

I have seen globalization's onslaught of cheap imported fruits and vegetables, and illegal and massive immigration simply destroy the agrarian world of the 1950s in which I grew up—including much of our own farm, lost to the bank because of poor prices and high costs. But I also appreciate that the local Wal-Mart—five minutes away from our doomed vineyard—is crowded with new consumers, recently arrived from Mexico. who drive Camrys and Civics purchased with easy credit, talk on cell phones for mere pennies, and reside in subsidized tract houses, with comforts superior to those found in more tasteful European homes. When I was in junior high school, summer jobs in town were prized and often meant a laborious apprenticeship under a hectoring small businessman who peered over your shoulder constantly as you tried to memorize his price tags and navigate through the maze of his ancient bronze cash register. Now, newly arrived clerks from Mexico at Jack-in-the-Box punch colored buttons with pictures of shakes and burgers and then instantly hand you a computer printout of your order—no dexterity, no languages, no skills needed other than physical and psychic resistance to the burdens of rote. The illegal alien makes fewer computing mistakes than I did three decades ago—and the "manager" is never really there, as his franchise seems to operate on autopilot and is monitored by videos far more percipient than any cantankerous boss of the past.

Our sophisticated and discontented in the universities are

also correct that American tastes spread insidiously, and like bad money drive out any competing expression that offers real contentment and transcendence. But these more discerning critics still are profoundly mistaken in suggesting that grasping corporations, through the evil of advertising and the lust for obscene profits, foist a depressing mass culture upon the people.

Would that this were the case, and that the popular culture could therefore be reshaped with a magic wand of regulations into something a little more tasteful, less shocking to a submissive populace. But the truth, instead, is that Americans find their movies, videos, bestsellers, Internet surfing, TV shows and magazine crassness immensely relaxing and entertaining as well as easily accessible. In short, it is all a shared addiction that inexorably builds affinity across racial lines, despite the best efforts of the sophisticates to tear such commonality apart.

What leftists have completely missed is that the greatest engine for social and cultural equality and harmony in America is the corporations they denounce—amoral entities that follow profits rather than allegiance to ideas, prejudices good and bad, or tradition. Jack-in-the-Box couldn't care less that its clerk at the window is of illegal status or dark hue, or has values that are very different from most native Californians. Nor does it care whether she talks with her car-bound customers, or whether she needs government money to supplement her minimum-wage earnings. If she has hands and legs that work, then she is like any other human in the world; and if her English is nonexistent, well, then the corporation can craft a machine of universal symbols to bypass that slight impediment for the nine hours she is on its watch.

In my own community, the great fans of Business-Max and Home Club are Hispanics, not fifth-generation Anglos who have the education, affluence and perhaps memories to support the local family-owned grocery and the town's beleaguered lumber store. The former are cheap, always open, and more likely to offer help in Spanish; the latter are discriminating, prefer quality to quantity, and may hold forth on the problems in the community as you purchase a can of paint.

We are at the last frontier of cultural democratization and limitless mass production, where for the first time in history, entertainment, fashion and media are economical, understandable, reachable and apparently enjoyed by everyone—regardless of race, age or gender. Whether this plethora of cheap goods and boorish entertainment derives from the labors of one billion Chinese who are now exporting their wares on the world market, or the ability to send satellite signals and the Internet into Amazon villages is unclear. What is indisputable is that the drudgery of the American workplace—forty full hours each week, with few European-style perks, and dismal wages for the uneducated—is ameliorated by cheap electronic goods, cheap clothes, cheap almost everything, spiced with sounds, images and tastes that are uniformly accessible and unifying. Europeans who drive their safe government cars to the beach, work seven hours a day, enjoy six to eight weeks off yearly, and have nearly all their medical problems, tuition, natal care and rest home worries taken care of by a maternal government see us as impoverished. Yet Americans find Europeans' tiny homes, solitary small cars, single televisions, and outrageously expensive food, clothes, entertainment and gasoline a real poverty that restricts the individual's ability to satisfy his cravings.

I used to roll my eyes when my parents turned on Perry Como and Frank Sinatra; today my children and I listen to Moby. My father and mother once complained that our clothes were too raggedy; our children now are likely to be dressed like us. My grandmother wore a pleated skirt and my grandfather wore railroad bib overalls; today my daughter and son wear each other's flannel shirts with unisex denim cutoffs, sometimes pilfered from my drawer. Just as age or gender distinctions have been absorbed by media and entertainment, so it is, at last, with race and national heritage—the last and most stubborn of man's traditional pecking orders to fall.

To the alien from Mexico, so often young and male, immediate inclusion into this new dynamic civilization has had a startling effect—perhaps deleterious to his moral development, to be sure; but for the purposes of immediate assimilation, on the other hand, undeniably good. Movies have sexy women of all colors. Images of a Hispanic Penelope Cruz dating Anglo Tom Cruise splash across magazine covers. The public cares little what color are Oprah, the Williams sisters, Tiger Woods, Jennifer Lopez (most recently engaged to Ben Affleck), Ricky Martin or Antonio Banderas. The only requisites for success in this glitzy culture are charm, athleticism, looks and pizzazz—none of it the property of any one ethnicity. If a Latina is curvy, she not only captures more attention than a rail-thin white woman—such universally human propensities and tastes are hardly new—but for the first time wins commensurate money, status and celebrity as a pinup in a world where the prejudices of the past are shown to be money-losers in the present.

The result is that millions of illegal aliens are seeing brown women and men arm in arm with blacks, Asians and whites at Food4Less and Starbucks, but also in limousines and giving celebrity interviews. Superficial equality? Perhaps. But again, for the first time in civilized memory all the old readily perceivable biases are simply vanishing—and that does affect a deeper reality. What class divisions we have are far more fluid than Europe's or Asia's. Money—a much fairer and more fluctuating barometer of status than birth and breeding—can put a prosperous cesspool franchiser on the local ballet board and lead his kids to be courted by the top universities.

This almost instantaneous blending of the social classes through shared cravings has, of course, nearly wrecked the efforts of immigrants to hold onto traditional Mexican life. I might complain that Chicano Dance instructors at my university are not providing our students with the necessary educational tools to succeed; they will lament in turn that their immigrant constituents are hopelessly hooked on rap music and would not be able to recognize a Mexican folk ballad without some instruction.

Consumerism in its most recent manifestation explains a great deal of the pathologies of second-generation Mexicans who grew up on violent video games, rap music, junk food, hanging at the mall, and without any of the strictures of traditional Mexican society such as the patriarchal family, church and extended kin. Yet for good or evil, the new America, unlike that even of the 1950s, now hardly objects to racial integration, intermarriage and open housing. What that means is there are almost no institutional barriers and few cultural impediments to assimilation—apart from those promoted by ideologues and intellectuals. While some Americans worry that illegal aliens are bringing their own culture up here, the aliens' extended families at home lament that *our* culture—even minus us—is down there.

My nephew and niece lost their Spanish at four years of age. They don't know anything now of their grandparents' village in Mexico. Their father was an illegal alien dishwasher; twenty-five years ago he took them to his Mexican village before granting custody to his ex-wife and her new husband, my twin brother. Both adults now, they date Anglos, South Americans, Asians and almost anyone they find attractive. They themselves are unsure whether they are half Mexican or half "white." And they don't care, anyway. If you told their friends that they were Spanish, Italian, Greek or Cuban, nobody would know the difference. My other brother's wife is Mexican-American; her father lives in Mexico City—and survives on his hard-earned American Social Security checks. Assimilation, in other words, through both intermarriage and shared consumerism, works. As far as I can tell, no one in my family as of yet has called for a *Republica del Norte.*

My neighbor is married to a Japanese woman; their daughter married a Mexican-American; their grandson—one-quarter Anglo, one-quarter Japanese, one-half Mexican—is now being raised by an Anglo stepfather. Nor is such racial complexity, a

Tiger Woods sort of amalgam, at all atypical in California, at least outside the faculty suburb. No wonder that the race industry is perplexed that its Neanderthal rubrics from the glory days of the 1960s ("check here for Anglo, Hispanic, non-Mexican Latino, African-American, etc.") increasingly make little sense to anyone. What all these people have in common is that their dress, patois and tastes are becoming more homogeneous. And these propensi-ties are predicated on the democratic principle that what is most accessible to the most people sells (the annual so-called Hispanic market represents $300 billion in sales), and what is not, doesn't. I used to hear Spanish ballads out in the fields, blaring on the radios of plum pickers. Such *campesinos* themselves wore khaki-like uni-forms with straw hats and said *"si señor—no señor"* when told to pick fruit by color or size. They looked and acted like the peasants in *The Treasure of the Sierra Madre.* Now the illegal alien plays ghetto-inspired rap, wears his baseball cap backwards, is amply tattooed, and is more likely to answer "OK already" or "No problema"—mimicking Schwarzenegger rather than speaking Spanish. I miss the old world; those in this new world would not.

If one were a small farmer trying to keep alive a traditional agrarian way of life for his children, if one were a third-generation Japanese small nurseryman struggling to survive amid a parking lot full of cheap plants at Orchard Supply, if one were proud of his Punjabi roots, religion, dance and customs and wished his daugh-ter to preserve an ancestral way of life drawn from a rich past in India, then the juggernaut of Blockbuster, Festival 10 Theaters, Pizza Hut, Costco, Borders Books, Amazon.com, MTV, Michael Jordan, Selena videos, *Judge Judy, Who Wants to Be a Millionaire?* and all that it represents would be maddening, even satanic in the way it destroys localism—and perhaps assaults nature itself. But if one were to come from dire poverty, oppression and racism in Mexico, then this same apparatus, by its very obliviousness to all distinct culture of the past, can turn a suspect outsider into a welcome insider within a few years. My best memories of the Bill Clinton sexual scandals were the amused smiles of illegal aliens at our nearby gas station as they snickered over tales of his phallic use of a cigar; they felt this was quite a country when their own sexual mores were superior to those of the President of the United States.

We should be clear about the limits of the assimilating culture, however. The illegal alien may marry a fourth-generation Anglo (as in the case of my sister-in-law), he may wear a Chicago Bulls cap and gyrate to punk rock, but that superficial immersion in American culture is no substitute for real civic education about American history, culture and values. But at least the leveling effect of popular culture does buy us a little time. It gives America a few years of respite before we must deal with the catastrophe that we are not educating millions, not teaching them a common and elevated culture, and not addressing the dilemma of open borders. But then we are not quite killing each other either, as happens daily in almost every multiracial society on the planet.

In the meantime, millions of Mixotec, Oaxacans and Indians from Jalisco and the Yucatan are very quickly becoming superficially similar to millions of white, Asian and African-American youth—a host generation that itself is increasingly illiterate, unskilled and ignorant of so much about the institutions and the very nature of its own country. If we in the 1940s and 1950s were once like Greece, with the local city-states' rich pride, culture, rigidity and baffling protocols for privileged citizens and those deemed inferior as metics and helots, we are surely now more like imperial Romans of Petronius's age, when all flocked to share without discrimination in the riches and occasional debauchery of a new global order.

In our eleventh hour of California's immigration woes, what gives us hope that we may all yet live as one harmonious people? It surely is not the federal government, which has lost control of its borders and placed immigration policy at the service of special interests, both here and abroad. It cannot be our California educational system, which has produced classrooms plagued by partisans and at the mercy of the teacher unions and the race industry, both so often hostile to a common culture. Another generation must pass before we can assess all the damage done by years of state-mandated bilingual education.

There is not a great deal of hope for assimilationist policies to be found in the professional Mexican-American leadership that thrives in government, journalism and the universities. Such elites more often seek preferences based not on their own claimed injuries, but on past bias against their fathers and hostility presently expressed toward illegals. Nor are there many state leaders who speak honestly about race, culture, immigration and the need for assimilation—not when California may soon find itself with half its population claiming Mexican heritage.

In our devil's bargain with the American-inspired globalism, we have exchanged standards and taste for raw inclusiveness—the age-old complaint, from Aristophanes to de Tocqueville, against democratic civilization. Yet racism, separatism and natural apartheid are *not* the dividends of the new music, videos and clothes. So until our attitudes about immigration, schooling and a common culture improve, for now the youth culture is proving to be virtually our only salvation—and so in a strange way we are lucky to have it.

EPILOGUE
Forks in the Road

 THE POOR OF THE WORLD are voting with their feet. Europe is awash with immigrants from northern Africa and the Middle East who now make up vast enclaves in England, Scandinavia and France. African blacks flock into a once racist South Africa still replete with tough and hateful Afrikaners. Refugees from a torrid Arabian landscape wait on lists to get into frosty Toronto. Hundreds of thousands of times more workers leave Palestine to find work in a despised Israel than Israelis—or Palestinians—venture into Syria or Lebanon. The freedom and material dynamism of the West are drawing millions to its shores—in the manner that Athens once attracted metics from Asia, and Rome drew Africans, Jews and Armenians. And just as in that distant past, today's new arrivals are unsure to what degree they wish to shed their old culture, language and customs. Most are confused over why they have abandoned countries they are unhappy with and yet find themselves uneasy with those they have chosen to embrace.

If Californians complain that the children of aliens claim they are Mexicans, not Americans, and cheer visiting Mexican soccer players while booing their American athletes, they should remember that Algerians do the same thing to their hosts in France, as Pakistanis often do in Great Britain, and as Turks in Germany. The freedom and affluence of the West affect both the poor Third World immigrant and the well-heeled Western host in a variety of strange ways. Americans and Europeans can develop a cynicism, boredom and smugness about their own soft society that suggests to perceptive aliens either a sense of outright self-loathing or at least an uneasy acceptance that patriotism, pride in one's culture and national solidarity have no place in a postmodern, postheroic West.

The immigrant, baffled by the strange new world with its unlimited freedom of expression, gender equality and competitive economy, is not baffled by this remorse on the part of his host. In fact, he is ready to exploit it. The result is that he often makes little effort to assimilate, and then blames the ensuing failure on precisely those whose sense of shame is assuaged by such hostility. The relationship for both is parasitic. The sophisticated white professor allays his fears and anxieties about race on the cheap by championing ethnic studies and bilingualism. (Yet he rarely wishes to live beside, marry among or spend the day with Mexican aliens and their offspring.) In turn, the opportunistic immigrant taps the host's guilt to explain his own easier choice of ethnic separatism and pride. "We owe these people/You people owe us" is now the new symbiosis, replacing the old honesty: "Join us if you wish to be like us/We wish to be like you, so let us join you." When students have identified themselves to me in ethnic terms as "Chicanos" (e.g., "As a Chicano, I say" or "We Chicanos believe"), I have replied with the corresponding, silly racial nomenclature, otherwise never employed in this way ("Yes, as a white person, can I help you?" or "We white people think"). In every case, the student immediately drops the self-identification, upset that anyone else should be so crude as to employ such a racial identity badge.

It is within this larger, global context of population movement—of people trying to leave the misery of poverty in Africa, Asia and South America to find hope in Western countries—that we too in the American Southwest find ourselves dealing with immigrants from Mexico. Let us also be honest about the nature of human traffic. It is not climate, natural resources or race that entices or repels immigrants to new shores. Rather the answer lies with the capacity of Western culture to create capital, provide security, offer freedom and emphasize the individual rather than the tribe. Wealthy Westerners, who prefer low birthrates so as to satisfy their appetites for leisure, freedom and wealth, invite in the poor from Africa, Asia and South America to join them, on the condition that they are willing to work immediately at menial jobs in exchange for some future chance to partake in a free and affluent society. But what starts out as a mutually beneficial relationship soon deteriorates into one of mutual recrimination and theater: the host hectors the immigrant that he is lucky to have escaped his nightmarish home; the new arrival barks back that he now wants near-instant parity with his employer and the right to romanticize his once hated homeland as salve for his wounded pride.

Truth alone is the beginning of remedy, and so we must begin with acceptance of the universal law that determines the direction of immigration. If we do not know why immigrants come, or for reasons of pride or chauvinism are too timid to discuss it, then we live in a doublespeak world and deserve the consequences.

America—and the Southwest particularly—is now unsure about the future. A choice of radically different potential fates awaits us, each predicated on choices we make in the here and now. Things can go very wrong for us if we continue to make poor decisions. The present immigration fiasco is not the result of any *one* past baneful idea, but arose solely because of the multiplier effects of several developments—many of them errors of omission and laxity rather than of deliberate intent. So let us conclude by reviewing the wide range of alternatives that might await us.

The really perilous course lies in preserving the status quo and institutionalizing our past failed policies: open borders, unlimited immigration, dependence on cheap and illegal labor, obsequious deference to Mexico City, erosion of legal statutes, multiculturalism in our schools, and a general breakdown in the old assimilationist model. True, the power of popular culture can superficially unite us and prevent the dangerous balkanization of the type we have seen in Eastern Europe, at least for a time. But we will still face a slow erosion in our general quality of life, and uncertainty that our group commitment to intermarriage, common popular icons and harmony in the youth culture will translate into a shared or elevated sense of national purpose.

Because too many unskilled Mexicans will come in numbers too great to be easily assimilated, and since their children will no longer be taught the need to accept the common protocols and heritage of American culture, the present pathology will only worsen. The United States will face—is in fact now facing—a terrible choice. Either we lower standards in our schools, businesses and government to ensure full participation by tens of millions who were never given proper education and training, or we maintain de facto a permanent class of modern helots who do the dirty jobs for their Spartan overlords, without ever joining fully in the management of the world that their hard work has helped to create.

If many of the current generation of illegal immigrants remains mired in stoop labor, their offspring will not be content with the solace that life is at least far better than it was in Mexico. Indeed, few sons and daughters of illegal aliens will know anything of Mexico. Millions will simply become jaded that their mothers and fathers work at jobs others won't take and yet make so much less—as they too enter the work force without education, at the bottom of the labor pool. We are all sitting on a demographic time bomb in which a shrinking, mainly white elite is nearing retirement and ready to be subsidized by more numerous, poorly compensated and younger Mexicans.

One solution would be to continue with de facto open borders, but insist on rapid cultural immersion, an absolute and immediate end to all ethnic chauvinism, bilingualism and separatism. There would have to be a domestic Marshall Plan to inculcate the norms and values of traditional education—a core curriculum that emphasizes the American heritage and unifies us through civic responsibility rather than divides us through an obsession with race. In this scenario, the inclusiveness of daily habit and custom, married with active support of a higher sort by our schools and government, might make near-instant citizens of thousands of illegal aliens. Even with the current of Mexican newcomers as it is, we could hope that their children had equal opportunity to enter the middle class. We might allow business cynically to maintain its access to inexpensive pools of unskilled labor. Thus in fifty years California would be a state of more than 60 or 70 million citizens, perhaps two-thirds of them of Mexican heritage. But such an identification would be of no particular importance precisely because the effects of total assimilation, intermarriage and ending government-sponsored separatism would have obliterated perceptible differences in income and education among Mexicans, whites, blacks and Asians.

This possible fate leaves the borders as they are, profits from the continued use of cheap labor and ignores illegality. It mitigates the social effects of a demographic free-for-all by returning to the old, proven assimilationist model of the nineteenth century, which Americanized millions of Poles, Irish, Jews and Italians, who also came to America without money and en masse.

Alternatively, we could patrol our border—to be sure, requiring fortification and a militarization of sorts—to ensure only legal and vastly reduced immigration, perhaps at a national rate of no more than 150,000 or so legal entries per year from Mexico. Business would have to accept a permanent scarcity of unskilled workers. Californians in turn would pay more for their hotel rooms, lawn care and fresh fruit—and have to do more of their dirty work themselves. In theory, American citizens without specialized skills would find themselves in far greater demand and would acquire greater leverage in negotiating more than minimum wages. Under conditions of such strict legality, illegal immigrants would have to be deported immediately. Controversy arising from offering tuition discounts and issuing driver's licenses to those who arrived illegally would disappear. Respect for the law would strengthen. Population growth would reach a natural equilibrium in California, perhaps forty million by the end of the new century.

As a trade-off for such vastly reduced immigration from Mexico, we would not worry so much about the multiculturalism taught in our schools. The fighting for inclusive standards and worry over a watered-down, feel-good curriculum would go on, but lose some of its intensity without the presence of millions of illegal newcomers. The La Raza dinosaurs, along with other separatists and ethnic chauvinists, might lumber on in theory, but in fact would gradually die off as their habitat became depleted of new clients and their landscape altered through the effects of intermarriage and the assimilative youth culture.

Within twenty or thirty years, Mexican ancestry would be comparable to Italian descent today. Cinco de Mayo would be no different from Columbus Day. Chicano studies professors, hobbling with canes and walkers, would scour the campus for a handful of Mexican immigrants they could imbue with distrust of America and its racist past—but for the most part encounter a completely assimilated third-generation student body who paid them little heed.

In short, we the hosts can either change our strategies about assimilating the immigrant flood or, alternatively, remain unchanged but dam the source of the deluge and do so under legal auspices. Either choice would radically alleviate the present problem within a few years. A third, more radical and holistic—and, I think, wiser—solution would be to adopt sweeping restrictions on immigration and put an end to separatist ideology along with the two-tier legal system for illegal aliens. In such a scenario, our present problems would vanish almost immediately, while prices for wage labor would steadily escalate.

There is, of course, a fourth approach—the logical culmination of the present policy—which leads to a true Mexifornia. If we do not change by either adopting an assimilationist program or insisting on metered and legal immigration, or both, we shall soon see a culture in southern and central California that really is a hybrid civilization, a *zona libre* not unlike what already exists in parts of inner Los Angeles and many rural California towns such as Orange Cove, Mendota, Malaga and Parlier. We know the warning signs of that rendezvous with tragedy for aliens when entire communities are Hispanicized. At present, 70 percent of the Los Angeles public school enrollment is reportedly Latino; only 10 percent is "white"—in large part because an entire middle and upper class has simply fled to private schools or more upscale public districts in the suburbs, practicing a self-interested apartheid even as it professes ideals of selfless liberality.

Under such a logical continuation of present policy, Spanish, de facto, becomes coequal with English; poverty becomes endemic; the federal and state governments replace the impoverished municipality as the salvation of last resort; schools erode; crime soars; and there seems to be little cultural opportunity for integration and Americanization. Many of those mired in these communities soon attempt to migrate to more integrated towns, as if it is not enough to make it across the border, but rather, real opportunity requires reaching towns that are not essentially simulacra of those found back in the Old Country—a pattern similar to other immigrant experiences from the very beginning of our history.

The Central Valley town of Parlier or Mendota could be the model for large parts of California if immigration remains unchecked. In that case, legal and illegal status becomes increasingly irrelevant for the basics of public life—college tuition, driver's licenses, welfare eligibility and perhaps soon even voting privileges. In the bilingualism that emerges, a new argot of Spanglish, neither Spanish nor English, is mastered as a language to be read and written with little real facility, while waves of newcomers, whether literate or not, demand or at least expect Spanish-only businesses and social services. Provocateurs in the race industry, government, and academia all rise up to meet the emerging opportunities offered by balkanization, giving ideological and political support to the idea of a true postmodern society without borders.

The performance of California schools sinks from the current dismal rank of 46th in the nation to dead last. Whites and Asians become increasingly bitter about having to accommodate their culture to millions of aliens, and African-Americans resent the erosion of entry-level wages and the gradual evolution of general racial preferences into more or less Hispanic and bilingual preferences. The state continues to run enormous deficits—perhaps twice the current annual $34 billion of red ink—as its budget doubles the present $100 billion in efforts to provide health care, remedial college courses, special tutoring, more law enforcement, widespread Spanish translation, and expanded prisons to meet the challenges of millions who continue to arrive illegally from Mexico.

So how would this new Mexifornia develop, if it takes root? I fear it would turn into an apartheid state that even the universal solvent of popular culture could not unite: an entrenched though shrinking white and Asian middle and upper class; a buffer group of assimilated and intermarried Mexican-Americans, whites and blacks; and dwarfing both of these, a large, unassimilated and constantly growing younger cohort of Mexicans, at odds with inner-city African-Americans. The California of today—the state with the highest number of Nobel Prize winners living amidst the highest rates of English illiteracy in the general American population—would morph into a new California without the Nobel laureates.

In such a future, the unskilled labor of illegal aliens fails to ensure a middle-class existence, but fuels the resentment to demand more government services and American privileges of the type that Mexicans south of the border could never envision. Our multicultural state would have the veneer of a new alternate identity; but in fact, it would combine the worst attributes of both nations, a dumbing-down of both languages, and radical and scary American individualism shorn of both the Anglo-Saxon-inspired allegiance to the letter of the law, and traditional Mexican familial and religious bedrock values. The law as we know it—in matters of citizenship, voting, legal status, driving and liability—would matter little, ignored when it proved inconvenient, turned to only *in extremis*.

Others look at California and see the nation's richest agricultural production, the embryo of the entire semiconductor and computer industries, Hollywood, favored tourist getaways, ideal weather, the infrastructure of a once great university system, oil, minerals and timber, key military bases and plants, busy ports— and America's most indebted state government amid social chaos. It is as if the wealthier our natural bounty and the richer the inheritance from our hardworking and creative forefathers, the greater the failure of the present generation that took so much and seems to be leaving so little.

What kind of fate do we want? In more placid times, this could be an academic question. But today we are at war with those who desire to kill us all, whatever the group we claim to belong to. The scab of our carelessness and inattention has been torn away, showing that the wound of separatism and ethnic conflict needs immediate care, lest it fester into disunity and thus weaken us when the stakes are so high. Yet there is some hope for salvation from the nightmare. Why? Because we got into our present mess only during the last thirty years and then only by doing almost everything wrong. To recover our state, our region and ultimately our nation, we still need not do *everything* right.